INTRODUCTION

TO

PSYCHOPATHOLOGY

INTRODUCTION
TO
PSYCHOPATHOLOGY

by *Shervert H. Frazier*, M.D.

PROFESSOR AND CHAIRMAN, DEPARTMENT OF PSYCHIATRY,
BAYLOR UNIVERSITY COLLEGE OF MEDICINE
DIRECTOR, HOUSTON STATE PSYCHIATRIC INSTITUTE

and Arthur C. Carr, Ph.D.

ASSOCIATE PROFESSOR OF MEDICAL PSYCHOLOGY, COLLEGE
OF PHYSICIANS & SURGEONS, COLUMBIA UNIVERSITY
ASSOCIATE CLINICAL PSYCHOLOGIST, NEW YORK STATE
PSYCHIATRIC INSTITUTE

Jason Aronson, New York

LIBRARY OF CONGRESS CATALOGING IN PUBLICATION DATA
Frazier, Shervert H
    Introduction to psychopathology.
    1. Psychology, pathological. I. Carr, Arthur C.,
joint author. II. Title. [DNLM: 1. Psychopathology.
WM100 F848i 1964a]
RC454.F7   1974   616.8'9'07   74-4368
ISBN 0-87668-141-0

To DR. LAWRENCE C. KOLB

With appreciation and gratitude

Foreword

This edition of *Introduction to Psychopathology* has been instigated by the receptive response to the volume which has come from students and workers in the field of mental health. Although the book was originally based on general lecture material prepared specifically for medical students in a course labeled "Psychopathology," it has proved a useful reference for students in nursing, education, social work, and psychology, as well as for others seriously interested in the study of human behavior. The clear, concise nature of the presentation has proved especially helpful in training paraprofessionals, the comprehensive group of workers who in recent years have come to make an important contribution to the management and treatment of individuals with psychologic or psychiatric distress.

The purpose of this volume is to introduce the student to a way of systematic thinking about psychopathology in terms of three particular frames of reference: classification, psychodynamics, and psychogenesis. Each of the major symptom types is discussed from these viewpoints, with relevant conclusions pertaining to its management. This organization has proved especially flexible in its applicability. The book has been used successfully as a text for formal courses, as a general background in psychopathology, as a preparatory aid for professional examinations, and as a basis for individual case presentation and discussion, as well as in the context of supplemental readings and more traditional textbooks in psychopathology, psychiatry, and abnormal psychology.

In organizing the material, the authors avoided making either a historical or a bibliographical survey. Aiming for a brief general presentation, they borrowed freely from the contributions of others. While the major sources are indicated in the bibliography, the authors felt that no personal disservice was implied by treating these contributions as being in the realm of general scientific information that may be discussed without specifically crediting the contributor.

Special appreciation is extended to Mrs. Alice Amberger and Mrs. Dora Friedman for their loyal secretarial services, as well as to Dr. Barry Wood and Dr. David Forrest who, as medical students, provided a watchful eye on the relevance of both expression and content. Dr. Austin Herschberger and Dr. Robert Liebert were also helpful in their criticism and comment.

Contents

1 INTRODUCTION   1

   Application of Terms   4
     CLASSIFICATION 5 ● PSYCHODYNAMICS 5 ● PSYCHOGENESIS 6

   Management   6

   Classification Supplement   7

2 DEPRESSIVE REACTIONS   9

   Classification   10
     NORMAL vs. PATHOLOGICAL 10 ● PRIMARY vs. SECONDARY
     DEPRESSION 10 ● NEUROTIC vs. PSYCHOTIC DEPRESSION
     11 ● EXOGENOUS vs. ENDOGENOUS 11 ● MANIC-DEPRESSIVE
     PSYCHOSIS 12 ● INVOLUTIONAL MELANCHOLIA 12 ●
     POSTPARTUM DEPRESSION 12 ● ANACLITIC DEPRESSION 13

   Psychodynamics   13

   Psychogenesis   16

   Summary   20

   Management   20

   Statistical Probabilities of Suicide   22

3 ANXIETY AND ANXIETY REACTIONS   23

   Classification   24
     NORMAL vs. ABNORMAL 24 ● ANXIETY vs. DEFENSES AGAINST
     ANXIETY 24 ● NEUROTIC vs. PSYCHOTIC 25 ● PHYSIOLOGICAL
     CONCOMITANTS OF ANXIETY vs. ORGANIC DISEASE 25

   Psychodynamics   25

   Psychogenesis   28

   Summary   30

   Management   31

4 PHOBIAS AND PHOBIC REACTIONS   35

Classification   36
NORMAL FEARS vs. PHOBIAS 36 ● PHOBIAS vs. PHOBIC
REACTIONS 36

Psychodynamics   36

Psychogenesis   41
EARLY FAILURES AT MASTERY 41 ● EARLY WITHDRAWAL PAT-
TERNS 41 ● REPRESSIVE INFLUENCES 42 ● PROJECTION 42

Summary   42

Management   43

5 BODILY EXPRESSIONS OF
     PSYCHOLOGICAL DIFFICULTIES   45

Classification   45
CONVERSION REACTIONS 46 ● PSYCHOPHYSIOLOGICAL DISOR-
DERS 47 ● HYPOCHONDRIASIS 47 ● OTHER BODY-IMAGE DIS-
TURBANCES 48

Psychogenesis   49

Psychodynamics   52

Summary   54

Management   55
CONVERSION REACTIONS 55 ● PSYCHOPHYSIOLOGICAL DISOR-
DERS 56 ● HYPOCHONDRIASIS 56 ● OTHER BODY-IMAGE DIS-
TURBANCES 56

6 OBSESSIVE REACTIONS   58

Classification   59
NORMAL vs. PATHOLOGICAL 59 ● OBSESSIVE PERSONALITY
60 ● OBSESSIVE-COMPULSIVE NEUROSIS 60 ● PSYCHOSIS AND
OBSESSIVE SYMPTOMS 60

Psychogenesis   61

Psychodynamics   62

Summary 66

Management 66

7 SEXUAL DISORDERS 68

Classification 69

Psychodynamics 71
HOSTILITY 71 ● DEPENDENCY 72 ● UNCONSCIOUS HOMOSEX-
UALITY 73 ● CASTRATION ANXIETY 73 ● MISPLACED IDENTIFI-
CATION 74

Psychogenesis 74

Summary 77

Management 77

8 DISORDERS OF CONSCIENCE 79

Classification 80

Psychogenesis 81

Psychodynamics 86

Summary 87

Management 87

9 DISORDERS OF INTELLIGENCE
   (MENTAL RETARDATION) 89

Classification 90

Etiology 92

Management 94

10 DISORDERS OF MEMORY, ORIENTATION,
    AND CONSCIOUSNESS 96

Classification   97
ORGANIC DISORDERS 98 ● FUNCTIONAL DISORDERS 99

Etiology of the Brain Disorders   101

Psychodynamics and Psychogenesis of Functional

Disturbances of Memory, Orientation, and

Consciousness   102

Management   104
BRAIN DISORDERS 104 ● FUNCTIONAL DISORDERS 104

11 PARANOID CONDITIONS   105

Classification   106

Psychogenesis   111

Summary   112

Management   113

12 SCHIZOPHRENIA   115
1. DISTORTIONS IN THINKING 116 ● 2. DISTURBANCES IN
AFFECT 116 ● 3. DISTURBANCES IN EGO BOUNDARIES 117 ●
4. DIFFICULTIES IN INTERPERSONAL RELATIONSHIPS 117

Classification   118
PROCESS vs. REACTIVE SCHIZOPHRENIA 118 ● SIMPLE SCHIZO-
PHRENIA 118 ● HEBEPHRENIC TYPE 119 ● CATATONIC TYPE
119 ● PARANOID TYPE 119 ● PSEUDONEUROTIC TYPE
120 ● SCHIZO-AFFECTIVE PSYCHOSIS 120 ● LATENT SCHIZO-
PHRENIA 120

Psychodynamics   121

Psychogenesis   123
GENETIC INFLUENCES 123 ● PHYSIOLOGICAL INFLUENCES
124 ● PSYCHOLOGICAL FACTORS 124

Summary   127

Management   128

13 PSYCHOTHERAPY   130

Common Elements of All Effective Psychotherapies 133

Supportive vs. Interpretative Psychotherapy   134
     SUPPORTIVE   PSYCHOTHERAPY   134 • INTERPRETATIVE
     PSYCHOTHERAPY 136

Appendix A Glossary   139

Appendix B Outline for Psychiatric History
   and Mental Status Examination   146

Appendix C Psychological Testing   150

Appendix D Bibliography   154

Index   163

1 〰〰〰〰〰〰〰〰〰〰〰〰〰〰〰〰〰〰〰〰〰〰〰〰〰

Introduction

Psychopathology has been defined variously as "the scientific study of mental disorders from the psychological point of view," [1] "the systematic investigation of morbid mental conditions," [2] and the "branch of science which deals with morbidity or pathology of the psyche or mind." [3] Less technically, it might be said that psychopathology is the study of the signs and symptoms of mental distress.[4]

---

[1] *Webster's New International Dictionary*, 2d ed., 1959.

[2] English, H. B., and English, Ava C. *A Comprehensive Dictionary of Psychological and Psychoanalytical Terms*. New York: Longmans, Green & Co., 1958.

[3] Hinsie, L. E., and Campbell, R. J. *Psychiatric Dictionary*. New York: Oxford University Press, 1960.

[4] In current usage, the term *psychopathology* unfortunately is sometimes also

This text will use as its initial data the symptoms of mental distress which either directly or indirectly bring a patient to a physician. Our entry into psychopathology will be largely in phenomenological terms, as it will deal with symptoms and discomfort experienced and reported by the patient. Our discussion will emphasize the role of such symptoms in the context of the patient's interactions with other people.

The following aspects of psychopathology will be considered: (1) classification, (2) psychodynamics, and (3) psychogenesis.

Classification is concerned with the categorization of the signs and symptoms of mental distress into meaningful groups or types. Unlike traditional diagnoses in clinical medicine, however, present classifications in psychopathology do not invariably bear a relationship to etiology. The complexities of human behavior have not yet yielded a nosology which invariably relates descriptive phenomena to causal factors, which in turn dictate specific treatment procedures. In some instances, classification conveys important distinctions which have implications for both treatment and prognosis; in other instances, its value rests largely as a device for communicative and statistical purposes. In either event, proper description and classification perform an important role in furthering some understanding of the disorder under consideration and may ultimately provide a basis for determining positive preventive measures.

Psychodynamics is concerned essentially with the functional significance of the emotional and the motivational aspects of behavior, including both conscious and unconscious determinants. A symptom is thus considered to be an expression of or the resultant of a constellation of forces presently operating within the person.

A basic assumption of psychodynamics is that behavior is goal-directed and motivated by impulses, needs, and forces of which the person is often not consciously aware. This implies that although man considers himself to be a rational being, he is frequently governed more by forces which he neither understands nor recognizes.

---

used as being synonymous with the symptoms themselves, e.g., "the patient's psychopathology." Correct usage would dictate the term "psychopathy" be used for this purpose, although its usage has also been tainted through incorrect association with "psychopath" and "psychopathic personality," terms of much more restricted meaning.

The rational explanations he gives for his behavior may bear little relationship to the motivations actually determining it. In fact, the "acceptable" conscious reasons for his behavior may even be in conflict with those which are outside his conscious awareness. Many symptoms can be viewed as a result of such conflict and the anxiety which the conflict precipitates.

An understanding of the individual patient's psychodynamics can usually come only through intensive exploration. A clarification of psychodynamics generally requires such techniques as direct observation, interview, biographical review of the person's life history, psychological tests, interpretation of dream and fantasy productions, and other less widely used methods of investigation (hypnosis, amytal interview, etc.). Nevertheless, in spite of the specificity of an individual's psychodynamics, abstractions and generalizations are possible which relate certain symptoms with their probable motivations.

Psychogenesis is concerned with the origin or the beginnings of the disorder, rather than with its present expression. As developed in the context of this volume, psychogenesis refers essentially to those life experiences which probably established the motivational patterns described under "psychodynamics." A fundamental assumption herein is that one's motivational patterns are established and derived primarily from early experiences, particularly those in the first five years of life.[5] This assumption does not deny that genetic or somatic factors may be important determinants of abnormal behavior, nor does it deny that later life experiences modify patterns of behavior established early in life. This assumption, however, does emphasize the early psychological or experiential factors which are believed to be correlated with the symptom under consideration. In many instances, the factors themselves may ultimately be proven to be re-

---

[5] Recognition of the importance of early life experiences in molding personality is generally accepted as one of Freud's major contributions. Few authorities would question today the effect of early experiences on later behavior, in spite of differences of opinion concerning all the relevant variables. Evidence for the long-lasting influence of early experience has been discovered in recent animal research, which demonstrates that there are indeed specific periods of heightened sensitivity in the young animal which have significance for all later social, intellectual, and emotional development. During these so-called "critical periods," the presence or absence of certain types of experience or learning has crucial effects on all that follows, particularly in the area of socialization.

lated to some other prior cause or etiology; hence, psychogenesis does not imply *ultimate causation*.

Our present understanding of the relationship between early life experiences and later psychopathy is based largely on retrospective historical data. In certain forms of psychopathy, early maladaptive patterns of behavior are perpetuated throughout life in repetitious and often obvious form; in other instances, early experiences seemingly establish a vulnerability which may not be apparent until symptoms are precipitated by a situation in life which in some way recapitulates or re-establishes early life difficulties. In studying such relationships, it must be recognized that the person is always the product of the interaction between his genic endowment and the environment in which he has lived. Except where there is specific organic pathology, however, psychogenesis attempts to specify the experiential contribution to the psychopathy under consideration.

APPLICATION OF TERMS

A brief example may suffice to clarify the distinction between the main terms used in this introduction. For this purpose, we will summarize a case described by Helene Deutsch: [6]

> A fifty-year-old authoress came into treatment suffering with an intense sadness and despair which had lasted for over a year, interrupted only by severe anxiety attacks. Basic to her verbalized complaints was the fear that she would be thrown on the street unclothed and suffer a lonely death. At times, she would scream for help and beg for pity; at other times, she would insist that she should be punished because she felt this was the fate she really deserved. The severe depression had begun with the loss of her dog, her prized possession, although the grief seemed even to the patient to be somewhat incompatible with the occasion.

Although the details described by Deutsch have been greatly abbreviated for our purposes, this summary will be adequate to clarify the distinction among classification, psychodynamics, and psychogenesis.

------

[6] Deutsch, Helene. *Psychoanalysis of the Neurosis*. London: Hogarth, 1932.

CLASSIFICATION

The patient's psychopathy could be categorized primarily as a prolonged and intense *depression,* with intermittent *anxiety attacks,* although the full history indicated other previous symptoms. For example, at an earlier time the patient had a recurring idea (*obsession*) that something would happen to her younger sister, and she repeated everything she did a certain number of times even though these acts appeared to be without meaning (*compulsion*). Because the patient's ability to test and evaluate reality was so poor, it appeared that her depression was of *psychotic* intensity. Systematic ordering of her symptoms into such classifications as "depression," "anxiety attack," "obsession," "compulsion," and "psychotic," although not the end in itself, is an important aspect of psychopathology.

PSYCHODYNAMICS

Investigation by Deutsch of the patient's symptoms revealed their *meaningfulness and significance in the context of the patient's motivations.*

> The patient's history revealed an early jealousy of a more beautiful and talented younger sister. Following the death of the mother, the patient at the age of twelve had been made responsible for the upbringing of this sister, a responsibility she undertook with the most solicitous care, ultimately even to the sacrifice of her own ambitions. For several years, the sisters lived in a mutually dependent relationship until the younger sister left the patient to marry and go abroad with her husband. The patient appeared pleased at the sister's happiness and adjusted calmly to the departure. Shortly after, she acquired a dog who became lost a year and a half later.

In the course of investigation, it was revealed that to the patient the dog was a surrogate for the lost sister and that its disappearance mobilized the grief which the patient had hidden within herself when the sister left. It was shown clearly that the self-accusations were really reproaches unconsciously meant for the ungrateful sister who had deserted the patient in spite of the patient's life of sacrifice. Among other purposes, the patient's suffering served as self-punishment for the intensely hostile feelings which she harbored toward the "dearly beloved" sister. Those students who are already familiar with the psychodynamics of depression will recognize the relevance of such concepts as *"ambivalence," "displacement"* and *"lost object."* Although the technical names for the processes reflected in the patient's behavior will be identified and defined later, a summary explanation of the motivational bases for the patient's symptoms is sufficient for the present to illustrate the concern of psychodynamics.

PSYCHOGENESIS

Our assumptions concerning psychogenesis will attempt to clarify the origins of the particular vulnerability which predisposed the patient to the intense reaction she experienced. It is to be granted that many people harbor unrecognized hostility to their sisters; nor is it uncommon for people to be saddened at the loss of a cherished pet. What were the origins of the exaggerated reaction which the patient evidenced?

Basic to our assumptions related to the psychogenesis of this particular reaction is the recognition that the differentiation between one's self and others is established during one's very early life, specifically during those very early experiences of the child with its mother. The patient, by punishing herself as she unknowingly wished to punish her sister, was reflecting a confusion and diffusion in her self-identity which in turn reflect disturbances in the early relationship with the mother. Those students who are aware of the most widely accepted theory of depression will recognize the relevance of such concepts as *incorporation, introjection,* and *identification.* Although we again shall not immediately define the processes by which we should explain the psychogenesis of the patient's depression, our hypotheses of "how the patient got this way" would be related to psychogenesis.

MANAGEMENT

It should probably be made explicit that effective treatment can sometimes be conducted without a thorough knowledge of either psychodynamics or psychogenesis. Some forms of therapy, such as various somatic methods of treatment, including drugs, may be initiated solely on the basis of the physician's knowing that the patient is depressed. Friendly support and understanding will sometimes themselves suffice to relieve a mild depression.

Treatment may also be based on a rational understanding of the patient's psychodynamics. Let us suppose, only for the sake of argument, that one could have arranged for the sister's marriage to fail, necessitating her return to the patient in a dependent, broken, helpless state. On the basis of the patient's psychodynamics, it would not be surprising to find that the patient might experience a sudden relief of her intense depression, assuming her responsibility with remarkable stoicism! However, a reinstitution of obsessions and compulsions would probably occur.

For the patient described above, Deutsch utilized psychoanalysis, a method of treatment which attempts to develop insight, a thorough understanding by a patient of his or her own motivations. The foundations of the patient's current psychodynamics were worked out in the context of a professional therapeutic relationship, and some understanding of the role of early child-parent relationships was developed. Many authorities believe this approach offers the best likelihood that the disorder will not recur.

Regardless of how he may attempt to alleviate a patient's mental suffering, the likelihood of success is greatly enhanced if the physician has a thorough knowledge of all aspects of psychopathology, including classification, psychodynamics, and psychogenesis.

CLASSIFICATION SUPPLEMENT

A *psychosis* is a severe disturbance in psychological functioning in which the individual's ability to distinguish, evaluate, and test reality is defective.

A *neurosis* is a disorder in which reality testing remains relatively intact but in which unconscious conflict gives rise to such symptoms as anxiety, feelings of depression, unreasonable fears, doubts, obsessions, and psychogenically determined physical ills.

A *character disorder* is distinguished by difficulties in conforming with cultural and social moral expectations with relatively little personal discomfort, and few or none of the major symptoms of a neurosis or a psychosis.

The major functional (i.e., nonorganic) psychoses are schizophrenia and manic-depressive psychosis. In *schizophrenia,* the major disturbance is reflected in a disorder of thinking and the thought processes. In the *manic-depressive* psychosis, the major disturbance is reflected in the emotional sphere, giving rise to depression, mania (elation and euphoria with overactivity), or both.

The major neurotic disorders are the obsessive-compulsive neurosis, anxiety neurosis, phobic neurosis, hysteria, and neurotic depression. In *obsessive-compulsive neurosis,* the major symptom is recurring ideas (obsessions) or acts (compulsions) which the individual feels compelled to perform. In *anxiety neurosis,* diffuse anxiety is the prominent symptom; whereas in *phobic neurosis,* anxiety and fear are elicited by a particular stimulus, e.g., high places, dirt, animals, etc. In *hysteria,* anxiety is converted into physical symptoms which have no organic explanation, e.g., blindness, paralysis, deafness, etc. In *neurotic depression,* feelings of depression constitute the major symptom.

2 ∿∿∿∿∿∿∿∿∿∿∿∿∿∿∿∿∿∿∿∿∿∿

Depressive

Reactions

One of the most common symptoms of patients who come to a physician is depression, a painful affect (subjective feeling state) characterized by feelings of sadness, discouragement, loneliness, and isolation. Sometimes such feelings are readily discernible in the patient's complaint that he feels sad, that he wants to die, that he feels like crying, or simply that he feels depressed. At other times, however, feelings of depression will be partially masked by more prevailing complaints related to weakness or lethargy, anorexia, inability to sleep, weight loss, general uneasiness, irritability, or numerous somatic complaints.

CLASSIFICATION

NORMAL VS. PATHOLOGICAL

The affect of depression may be present in any number of clinical syndromes, ranging from normality to psychosis. Depressive feelings may be appropriate to and commensurate with the situation eliciting the reaction, as in a normal grief response. Such instances are usually short-lived and are not accompanied by any great loss of self-esteem. Following a period of mourning, the individual becomes free to resume comfortable living. In depression as a pathological phenomenon, however, the reaction is of an intensity or duration which is not appropriate to the occasion, even when a precipitating factor is prominent.

The severely depressed patient may be uncommunicative and unresponsive. His outlook is gloomy and morbid. He finds life dull and uninteresting. As his depression becomes more intense, there may be a motor retardation and a slowing of thought processes. He may sit for long periods of time in one position, with head drooped, and with apathetic or mournful facial expression. He may frequently sob or sigh. His verbalizations reflect his sadness, hopelessness, lack of pleasure in life, low self-esteem, feelings of emptiness, and excessive self-preoccupation, and are often accompanied by bodily complaints which seem as real as if they had an organic substrate in the form of a disease process. He may be preoccupied with regrets for past mistakes (real or imagined) and express shame, guilt, and self-reproach. Feelings of failure and worthlessness are common, often related to "misdemeanors" more relevant to a child's behavior, e.g., being "dirty" or "bad." If not retarded in movement, he may be extremely agitated, with pacing, handwringing, and restless distress.

PRIMARY VS. SECONDARY DEPRESSION

Depressive feelings may accompany any form of psychopathy, arising either as a reaction to it or superimposed upon it; e.g., an obsessive-compulsive neurotic may become depressed when he is not achieving in life. In such instances, depression is secondary to the more basic disorder. However, depression may constitute the basic disorder giving rise to the clinical syndrome of *depression*, per se. Although the presenting symptom in both instances may be the depressive affect, the clinical syndrome of depression invariably also includes multiple somatic complaints (fatigue, insomnia, eating difficulties, constipation, motor retardation, or agitation) and loss of self-esteem (self-accusatory and self-depreciatory ideas, frequently with feelings of guilt). Since the depressive affect in either state sometimes can be relieved relatively easily, the distinction between primary and secondary depression carries prognostic implications for what will remain after this affect is alleviated.

NEUROTIC VS. PSYCHOTIC DEPRESSION

In the clinical disorder of depression, it is important to distinguish whether the patient's ability to test and evaluate reality is intact (generally so in a neurotic depression) or whether reality testing is seriously disrupted (psychotic depression). This distinction is sometimes difficult, since depressed patients are often uncommunicative and may not immediately reveal disorders in their thinking processes. In psychotic depression, delusions (false beliefs) and hallucinations (false sensory impressions) are often present and frequently relate to the body or bodily functions. Hospitalization is almost always necessary for a psychotic depression.

EXOGENOUS VS. ENDOGENOUS

Depressions are sometimes classified as either exogenous or endogenous. *Exogenous* refers to depressions precipitated by discernible events in the environment to which the person responds. *Endogenous* depressions, on the other hand, refer to those depressions which are without obvious external precipitation, appear to arise spontaneously, and tend to be more recurrent. Some authorities feel that this distinction is an artificial one, believing that most depressions, upon close inspection, can be demonstrated to be a reaction to some change (or loss) in the person's real or imagined world. Others give greater emphasis to the role of constitutional and genetic factors as determinants of all depressive reactions.

MANIC-DEPRESSIVE PSYCHOSIS

The syndrome of manic-depressive psychosis is characteristically a recurrent or cyclical disorder that occurs for the first time in the twenties or early thirties. Some patients have only depressive episodes occurring at either unpredictable or regular intervals. In some patients, depression alternates with manic episodes characterized by flight of ideas, hyperactivity, and elation. Other patients have only manic episodes. Any alternation of these cycles may occur in the same patient. Manic-depressive episodes usually occur in individuals who throughout life have been outgoing but who experience varying mood swings and energy levels. Perhaps more than with any other kind of depressive reaction, manic-depressive psychosis is assumed by many to have a strong genetic determinant. Evidence for this assumption is the cyclical nature of the disorder, often without apparent external cause, and the high incidence in some families.

INVOLUTIONAL MELANCHOLIA

This is a severe depression of psychotic intensity occurring at the time of the climacteric in individuals without previous history of a manic-depressive reaction. Delusional ideas are common, frequently in reference to the body or bodily functioning. Much agitation and anxiety are also present. Individuals developing this disorder have been frequently shown to be highly compulsive, "driven" individuals throughout life. Some authorities believe that a disequilibrium in endocrine functioning may lay the basis for this reaction; others think the psychological meaning of the climacteric is the more significant factor.

POSTPARTUM DEPRESSION

This depression in women usually occurs three weeks to three months after childbirth. Panic, fear, depression, and feelings of inadequacy in handling the newborn are frequent aspects of the syndrome. Although previously thought to be an organically determined disorder, it has been increasingly recognized as a functional illness which occurs in response to the threat of motherhood.

ANACLITIC DEPRESSION

A response in an infant to the sudden loss of mothering is characterized by loss of interest in the environment, withdrawal, loss of appetite, insomnia, apprehension, and a physiognomic expression, all of which, if occurring in an adult, would be interpreted as depression. This response, which can be demonstrated simply by withdrawing motherly attention from the child, is accepted by some authorities as support for the contention that all later depressive reactions are recapitulations of this kind of loss and are psychogenic rather than organic in origin.

Psychodynamics

People who become pathologically depressed tend to be highly conscientious, rigid individuals who are conventional in their thinking and dependent in their behavior. They tend to dichotomize all aspects of living into black or white alternatives. Their conscious motivations are usually above reproach. It is often precisely because of the high standards these people set for themselves and others that they ostensibly become disillusioned and depressed.

Perhaps the most generally accepted psychodynamic explanation of depression is derived from the fact that the depressive affect is not qualitatively different from that which occurs in a normal *grief* reaction. The similarity of feelings accompanying normal grief and those accompanying the clinical entity of depression is taken to support the impression that underlying all depression is the experience of a *loss*. Behind the frequent complaints of a depressed patient, one can, in fact, detect his feeling that something has been taken away from him. The common situations in which this occurs are the loss of a loved one, the loss of a job, the loss of money, social failure, diminished self-esteem, changes in the body-image, or loss of health. The loss may be real or imaginary, however. Sometimes it is only an *imagined* threat of a loss that precipitates the emergency situation. This loss, which may be related to a person, thing, value, or idea, is subsumed in the expression "lost object," or "lost love-object." Close inspection of the relationship of the patient to the "lost object" frequently reveals that it is invested with *ambivalence.*

Ambivalence: *coexistence of opposing feelings, usually involving both love and hate.*

Ambivalence is sometimes revealed in normal mourning when inadvertent expressions of anger and resentment toward the deceased will exist simultaneously with expressions of deeply felt grief. In a relationship when a person has extreme ambivalence which he does not consciously recognize or cannot accept, he is vulnerable to more inappropriate reactions when the relationship is disrupted. The intensity of underlying ambivalence is often not immediately apparent, since it is difficult for such contrasting feelings to coexist simultaneously in the patient's conscious awareness. Nevertheless, the role of underlying feelings of anger and resentment in the psychodynamics of the depressive reaction is so significant that it leads to one formulation of depression as being essentially a reflection of "retroflexed rage" (anger turned against the self).

It sometimes appears that the loss would not warrant the intense reaction it precipitated. When the depressive reaction appears highly incompatible with the precipitating loss, it may be assumed that a *displacement* of feelings is occurring.

Displacement: *the process by which an emotion or feeling is unconsciously transferred from its object to a more acceptable substitute.*

Feelings thus may be experienced as related to an object other than the one that is actually the focus of the fused ambivalent feelings.

As was revealed in the case referred to in Chapter 1, the patient became depressed at the loss of her dog, although the feelings precipitated were actually related to the earlier loss of her sister.

Although the patient was aware only of her deep love for the sister, the relationship was one of marked ambivalence because of the resentment over past sacrifices which the patient had made for her sister.

Discerning the complexities of the psychodynamics of a patient's depression is complicated further by other psychological maneuvers used by the patient to adjust to a real or imagined loss. For example, in some patients, *denial* may also be used in varying degrees and in alternating cycles.

Denial: *a process involving the avoidance of a painful or anxiety-producing reality by refusing to admit its existence. This process is unconscious; upon confrontation, the patient is unaware of the painful affects which are being denied.*

In mild form, denial results in an exaggerated sense of well-being, which is suspect only by virtue of its inappropriateness to the surrounding circumstances. Denial may also be so intense as to give rise to a state of *mania*. The ease with which such a state can be dissolved into a tearful depression, sometimes merely by confronting the patient with significant aspects of his reality, demonstrates the close relationship between depression and mania.

An industrial executive decided that he had just finished being depressed and was having relief from "all this terrible depression." He went to a boat show and became elated at what he saw. He decided he wanted the largest boat in the place and immediately wrote a check for it. He then suggested to the salesman that he needed a variety of accessories, since boating was an entirely new venture for him. He wrote checks for everything he selected. Upon his return to the hospital that night, he was asked how he felt, and he replied, "Oh, fine, doctor. I never felt better in my life. I had a wonderful day. I decided I'm going to boat all summer." The next morning, however, he awakened severely depressed. He was desperate. When it was pointed out to him what he had done, he said, "Yes. I don't want that boat. I have no need for it whatsoever."

The depressive reaction is essentially a cry for help, a plea for someone to "'do something for me," a bid for love, service, and attention. The strong underlying wish to be dependent may ultimately irritate other people. In fact, it appears as if the patient's behavior is partially motivated by the desire to do just this, although the patient has no awareness of such a wish. The patient often takes the irritation of other people graciously, since it confirms what he thinks of himself. Because satisfaction of his wishes for dependency gratification is not realized, the patient comes to the awareness that nobody will provide help which will magically cure him, and he may then become further consumed by feelings of sadness, hopelessness, fear, anger, and guilt.

PSYCHOGENESIS

There is some evidence that the crucial experience, which forms the basis for later depressive reactions, centers around the child's early feeding experience and his adjustment to the loss of the mother. Some authorities believe it is specifically the breast (or breast substitute) which constitutes the earliest significant loss; others believe it is more generally the mother herself and the change which occurs in the total "mothering" relationship.[1]

Prolonged psychoanalytic investigations of patients with severe depressions support the contention that the reaction to weaning and the struggles which follow may set the model for later reactions to other losses. Evidence for the contention that such early problems set the pattern for later depressive reactions is also found in the frequency with which depressed patients have difficulty with eating, manifesting conflict over food. Some depressed patients express complete lack of interest in any food. Other patients tend to overeat when they are depressed. In some instances, it appears that eating serves as a method of reassurance against underlying feelings of loss, deprivation, or depression.

---

[1] Psychoanalytic theory has traditionally stressed the oral dependency aspects of the early child-mother relationship. Recent research on "critical periods" in animals, however, suggests that tactile and other aspects of the total mothering relationship may be of previously unsuspected importance in relation to later patterns of development.

Early separations from the mother's breast represent a crucial experience in the development of a young infant. The experience of "weaning" derives its importance not only from the fact that it is related to the child's basic need for nourishment, but also to the child's adjusting to temporary separations from the mother. At this time, the child is also in the process of learning the distinction between that part of the world which is "him" and subject to his control, and that part which is "not him" but rather someone or something else. This process has been referred to as learning to differentiate the "self" from the "nonself," [2] a differentiation which is basic to the later establishment of a firm sense of self-identity or ego boundaries, as well as to the later development of adequate reality testing.

In view of both the satisfactions and frustrations experienced by the child, his relationship to the breast (mother) may be extremely ambivalent, as the weaning process confronts the child with his own helplessness in relation to the unobtainable aspects of life and reality. This ambivalence is sometimes revealed in the biting behavior which becomes prominent as the child develops teeth. To the immature child, means of retaliation are limited. Swallowing, or "oral incorporation," provides the primary means by which the child attempts to hold on to an elusive or frustrating object. The earliest means of adjusting to a possible loss is attempting (either in fact or fantasy) to hold onto the object by incorporating it, an act which eliminates the boundaries between the person and the desired object. Unconscious fantasies of incorporation may persist throughout adulthood and have been found to underlie disorders such as certain types of homosexuality and alcoholism.

The depressed person, when reacting to the emergency created by a loss, is utilizing methods of adjustment similar to those used by the young child in adjusting to his first major loss. The patterns by which these similar reactions are perpetuated are generally subsumed under the concepts of *incorporation, identification,* and *introjection.*

---

[2] This distinction subsumes numerous finer differentiations which the child learns through early experience in the context of his rapidly changing developmental level—mother vs. not-mother, human vs. nonhuman, animate vs. inanimate, male vs. female, etc.

Incorporation: *the process of taking something into oneself.*

In a young child, this process of incorporation pertains more directly to what is literally taken in through the mouth. In the course of normal development, the term is more applicable in the figurative sense, referring to the taking in of attitudes, knowledge, and values, as a basis for *identification.*

Identification: *the process of becoming like something or someone in some aspect of thought or behavior, based on an* **internalization** *of the* **image** *of the external object.*

As a mode of normal adjustment, identification serves as the means by which a boy, for example, accepts and assimilates patterns established by his father; the girl likewise identifies with the mother. Identification can be used to adjust normally to a loss, as is sometimes revealed in the course of mourning when the bereaved unconsciously adopts mannerisms or characteristics which were those of the dead person. In some instances, he will develop physical symptoms similar to those accompanying the fatal illness of the dead person. The bereaved person (after some attempts motivated by the desire to bring back the lost person) will also retain a link to the lost object through fond memories, recollections, and perhaps even through symbolic representations of the person in the form of preserved possessions. With the passage of time, the person becomes free to seek some other replacement. Such a mature use of identification as a means of adjusting to a loss is possible only when a sense of self-identity (or firm ego boundaries) has been established before the loss.

Introjection: *A less adaptive and more primitive way of adjusting to a loss than that which characterizes the process of identification, although sometimes used synonymously. In introjection, the "object" is "incorporated" but is neither integrated and assimilated into the personality through the more mature process of identification nor is it ever fully relinquished. A fusion of ego boundaries occurs between the* *self and nonself (the incorporated image or object), since the ability to make this distinction was never adequately developed.*

In a reaction to a loss which results in a pathological depression, processes are analogous to those involved in incorporation and *introjection* rather than to incorporation and *identification*. The introjection of an object toward which there was intense ambivalence gives rise to depression, self-accusations, and feelings of worthlessness which reflect the previously unacceptable aspects of the original relationship. That is, the ambivalence, originally directed to the incorporated object, is now expressed against the self because the object and the self are not distinguished. The self-accusations of a depressed person can thus be the unconscious accusations the person is directing at someone else (the incorporated object).[3] In his cry for attention, love, and service, the person may also be acting out his unconscious desire to punish someone else. Further guilt and depression ensue.

> In the case referred to in Chapter 1, it will be recalled that the patient feared the possibility of being thrown onto the street where, lonely and deserted, she would die a miserable death. This fear alternated with the feeling that this was the fate she deserved. Such accusations were understood as reflecting the fate she unconsciously felt the ungrateful sister deserved. If the patient's own ego boundaries (self-identity) had been firmly established, such a fusion and confusion could not have occurred, regardless of how unappreciative the sister may have been.

The processes of incorporation, identification, and introjection may appear to be rather fanciful descriptions of hypothesized fantasies and events. Nevertheless, the validity of these processes has been demonstrated in the dreams and fantasies of disturbed patients. Their clinical usefulness is especially apparent in understanding the disorder of depression.[4]

---

[3] In an extension of this formulation, some authorities would interpret constipation, a frequent complaint of the depressed patient, as an inability to give up the ambivalent object. The retention of this ambivalent object may, in a depression of psychotic intensity, give rise to bodily delusions involving ideas of being "dead" inside or "rotting away."

[4] The authors' discussion of early childhood experiences has emphasized the

SUMMARY

The following assumptions are helpful in understanding a depressive reaction:

1. Underlying every depressive reaction is the experience of a loss, whether it be a person, thing, idea, or ideal ("lost object").

2. In an abnormal reaction to such a loss, it can be assumed that the relationship to the lost object was highly ambivalent.

3. The tendency of certain individuals to experience abnormal reactions to such a loss is assumed to be related to a pattern established at the time of the reaction to the first loss.

4. The despair, suffering, and self-accusations apparent in a depressive reaction may represent retributions unconsciously desired for the "incorporated" lost object, as well as representing self-punishment for the harboring of unconscious ambivalent wishes toward that object.

5. Depression is a cry for help, a bid for service and attention, a plea that someone "do something." Its end result may also serve to punish others.

6. In spite of its marked contrast to the depressive state, mania is closely related to depression and can be understood as the *denial* of a depressive affect.

MANAGEMENT

Recent advances in pharmacology have made it possible to modify the intensity of a depressive reaction through the use of antidepres-

---

significance of so-called "oral" functions in the child. Some authorities would also emphasize the role of anal- and bowel-training problems, stresses which occur somewhat later in the child's development than do the problems centering around weaning. Among those who accept the role of early childhood experiences in the genesis of later depressive reactions, however, there is a general agreement that the major disruptive experiences have occurred at a later stage in the development of the child's interpersonal relationships than is the case in the disorders labeled "schizophrenia."

sant drugs. Other somatic means, particularly electroconvulsive therapy, may dramatically relieve intense depressive reactions. Patients can thus be helped by means that do not directly involve dealing with the psychodynamics of the disorder.

In brief psychotherapy, it is wise to concentrate exploration on the present life experiences of the patient, without reference to the etiological origins of the disorder. In some instances, the ambivalence is sufficiently close to awareness that ventilation of the patient's anger is possible. Such an expression, in the context of a warm supportive relationship, may bring relief, even in the absence of any insight on the patient's part.

Long-term psychotherapy has as its goal the significant change of enduring lifelong patterns of adjustment which give rise to the disorder. Psychotherapy is made difficult by the fact that these patients, when they are no longer feeling depressed, generally are not introspective and do not feel much need for personality change. In therapy, such patients demonstrate a clinging dependency which many therapists find extremely difficult to tolerate. Nevertheless, highly successful results with psychotherapeutic treatment have been reported.

It must also be recognized that many depressed patients will evidence spontaneous improvement. It sometimes appears as if the depression runs its course when sufficient expiation is obtained in the form of self-punishment for harboring ambivalent feelings. In general, depressive reactions have a favorable prognosis, barring possibility of self-destruction. Recurring episodes are also likely.

One possibility which must always be considered with depressed persons is *suicide*. To evaluate this risk, one must keep in mind the patient's need to obtain a response, the depth of his depression, the total affect of the patient, his capacity for accomplishing self-assertive behavior, his past history, as well as his fantasies of "What will happen if I do attempt suicide?" When judging the suicidal risk in a person, it is important to obtain the substance of the "rescue fantasy," i.e., "Who is going to take care of me if I attempt it?" From statistical studies on suicide, it is recognized that the majority of persons who make suicidal attempts or who do commit suicide try to warn someone of what they are about to do.

STATISTICAL PROBABILITIES OF SUICIDE

Age: Greater frequency at teenage and involutional periods of life.

Sex: Although more women attempt suicide, more men accomplish the act.

Health: Chronic medical illness increases the likelihood of suicide.

History: Suicide of a significant person (usually a parent) in the patient's life increases the likelihood of suicide.

Stage of
  illness: Generally occurs when the patient is recovering from the depth of his depression and may appear to be substantially improved.

3

Anxiety and

Anxiety Reactions

Expressions of anxiety, either in manifest or disguised form, frequently constitute the complaint which brings the patient to the physician.

Anxiety: *an affective state characterized by feelings of apprehension, uncertainty, and helplessness which are not attached to a real external danger.*

As a subjective feeling state, anxiety is exceedingly uncomfortable and often intolerable. With physiological manifestations similar to those of fear, it may arouse symptoms of a hyperactive sympathetic system which include perspiration, tremor, diarrhea, vomiting, "tightness in the chest," and changes in pupillary response, heart beat, pulse rate, and respiration. Unlike fear, however, anxiety is an unexplainable, pervasive feeling of impending disaster which will frequently be described as, "I'm afraid but I don't know why"; "I have a feeling that something is about to happen, but I don't know what"; "It's like a feeling of impending doom, but I don't know what it's about"; "I feel as if I'm about to explode or burst"; or "I feel I'm going to lose control." Behind these complaints is the implicit feeling of uncertainty and helplessness, which in extreme form may give rise to panic and disorganized behavior.

CLASSIFICATION

NORMAL VS. ABNORMAL

Like the depressive affect, anxiety is present in many disorders. In our culture with its many inherent conflicts and dangers, a certain degree of anxiety is perhaps both normal and desirable. Anxiety may serve a useful purpose by motivating the individual to productive goal-directed behavior. However, it may also reach extreme proportions, be extremely disorganizing, and lead either to a paralysis of behavior or to random, uncontrolled activity.

ANXIETY VS. DEFENSES AGAINST ANXIETY

Anxiety may play a dual role, serving either as a symptom in and of itself or as a motivating force for other symptoms. Because directly experienced anxiety is an exceedingly unpleasant feeling, the individual tends to develop *defenses* to avoid it or to mitigate its effects. These defenses mirror patterns of adjustment which have been developed in the course of life and reflect the total adaptive capacities of the individual. Although such defenses originally were truly "defensive" (protective) in the sense that they helped escape the effects of directly experienced anxiety, they may develop into extremely constricting forms of psychopathy. According to this view (the anxiety theory of neurosis), many neurotic and psychotic symptoms are considered as defenses against anxiety.

NEUROTIC VS. PSYCHOTIC

Defenses are usually only partially successful in eliminating the effects of directly experienced anxiety. Thus, overt anxiety is usually present in both neurotic and psychotic disorders. In "anxiety states" or "anxiety reactions," the distinguishing characteristic is that anxiety exists in relatively unmitigated form, without the development of defenses which would give rise to other predominant symptomatology. These disorders are in the *neurotic* classification since no gross distortion in reality testing occurs. Overt anxiety also can be present with other clinical symptomatology (depressive, phobic, compulsive, psychotic, etc.) which, if dominating the clinical picture, establishes the diagnosis accordingly.

PHYSIOLOGICAL CONCOMITANTS OF ANXIETY VS. ORGANIC DISEASE

Anxiety typically includes physiological manifestations which may be mistaken for organic disease. Hence, it is important to distinguish the somatic pattern which accompanies anxiety (involving the cardiovascular and gastrointestinal systems in particular) from other organic pathology.

PSYCHODYNAMICS

Although our discussion will stress the interpersonal aspects of anxiety reactions, there is perhaps no psychic phenomenon which is more multidimensional in its origin and its expression than the emotion of anxiety. Recent experimental evidence suggests that one's reaction to emotional emergencies or threat are related to dispositional tendencies which are determined by a combination of both biological and psychological factors. Experimental stress, for example, has been shown to elicit quite different cardiovascular responses in individuals, differences which are apparently related to genetic and innate biological factors in addition to early childhood experiences and the individual's present perception of the situation in which he finds himself. In discussing the psychodynamics of anxiety reactions, we are dealing with environmental precipitants of an extremely complex reaction.

From the psychodynamic viewpoint, a characteristic of any anxiety reaction is the fact that something in the present is precipitating a response pattern which harks back to the time when the individual was really helpless. In this sense only, anxiety is "irrational," since it is precipitated by something in the present which reactivates memories or conflicts of the past. A reaction appropriate to the original threat is now elicited by the present situation which reactivates childhood fears of loss of love, of separation, and of punishment, with accompanying feelings of helplessness.

There are, of course, "situational neuroses" in which present factors are important enough to produce the anxiety in the present time and place: "war neuroses" might be an example of this kind of reaction. Usually, however, the present situation elicits anxiety largely because it unconsciously reactivates memories of earlier conflicts.

The precipitating threat in an anxiety reaction usually arises in the patient's present relationships with other people which in some way jeopardize his established set of operations that in the past served to ward off punishment or the loss of love. This threat is frequently symbolic in nature, representative of a danger not directly known to the patient. Hence, unlike that which occurs in a fear reaction in which the source of the danger is recognized, the feelings of apprehension that arise in an anxiety reaction often appear to be without adequate rationale or logical basis, particularly to the patient himself whose sense of helplessness is thus only further intensified.

Any threat that jeopardizes the individual's established way of relating to others and that places him in conflict in terms of his own value system can give rise to anxiety. Superficially, it may appear that the kinds of situations which elicit such threat are legion, involving problems of disapproval, failure, disgrace, self-satisfaction, guilt, integrity, self-sufficiency, more basic to which are the individual's need to maintain a certain image of himself. Upon closer inspection, these situations would generally seem to have in common the emergence of unacceptable impulses related to (1) sex and/or (2) aggression, impulses which in childhood were met by either the threat of punishment or the loss of love.

> A twenty-five-year-old male appeared at an internist's office complaining of rectal itching. After a physical examination, he felt a full feeling in his rectum and wondered aloud whether the doctor had harmed him. Three days later, just prior to another physical examination, the patient experienced an acute anxiety attack, with physical manifestations so extreme that brief hospitalization was necessary. Investigation subsequently indicated strong underlying homosexual impulses against which the patient was defending himself, impulses triggered off by the physician's rectal examination which the patient found physically both enjoyable and painful.

> While out walking in the street, a young mother saw a child almost hit by a car. At this time, she experienced only feelings of relief that the car had stopped in time. Two days later, while tending her own crying child, she was suddenly overcome with anxiety and began shaking and perspiring profusely. In consultation, she now remembered "for the first time" that when the near-accident occurred, her thought was "What if that were Betty?" (the name of her own baby). Her relationship to her own baby was an extremely ambivalent one, generally characterized by overly solicitous care and attention. Exploration of her own feelings about the child modified her recall of the near-accident at which time her fleeting thought was closer to "I wish Betty were dead."

In individuals who are prone to anxiety attacks, unacceptable sexual and aggressive thoughts, feelings, and impulses are ordinarily handled by *repression*.

Repression: *the exclusion from awareness (or consciousness) of threatening impulses, feelings, memories, or experiences.*

Utilizing repression, one simply fails to see, to hear, to attend to threatening stimuli, whether they arise in terms of internal pressures (intolerable wishes, impulses, or ideas) or external threats (emanating more directly from other people). This process goes on unconsciously; the person is no more aware of repressing something than he is of forgetting something. Unlike simple forgetting, however, repressed material continues to seek expression, through derivatives which often are expressed in the form of other symptoms.

Repression is a ubiquitous defense in the sense that everyone expends some energy in keeping many unacceptable impulses and their derivatives out of conscious awareness. In some individuals, however, repression is found to be the primary and overriding aspect of defensive strategy. Although leaving the individual perennially immature, naive, and unreflective, repression may still succeed in working tolerably well, protecting the individual from experiencing excessive anxiety. In certain situations, repression fails to serve this purpose, either because of the nature of the external threat facing the individual or the nature of internal pressures arising from intolerable wishes. The failure of repression then gives rise to directly experienced feelings of anxiety and possibly the physical manifestations as well.

PSYCHOGENESIS

The child has his first experience of anxiety in his initial attempts to deal with other people as well as in attempts to handle his own impulses of sex, hostility, and greed.[1] He begins to feel that he cannot survive when he becomes aware that his existence is dependent on

---

[1] Although theoretical concepts of the primal source of anxiety vary, some authorities feel that birth is the prototype of all later traumatic and anxiety-producing situations. However, the disorders referred to as "anxiety," "phobic," and "hysterical" reactions were traditionally conceived of as defenses against impulses which do not become prominent in the young child until the ages of three to five years (namely, genital, oedipal impulses). Indeed, the precipitating incidents in such reactions often appear to be sexual in nature. Nevertheless, more recent concepts of anxiety would suggest that all anxiety reactions in some way signify a threat of loss of love and support, a threat originally emanating in our culture from the mother figure. Consistent with this view, the disorders described above invariably manifest strong dependency problems, suggesting that anxieties already existed in the mother-child relationship prior to the period at which genital and oedipal impulses first appear.

the actions of someone over whom he may have relatively little control and upon whom he is dependent for love and support. It is postulated that the child at this time experiences fear and requires the reassurance of the mothering person to alleviate the anxiety and fear about survival which, because of his helplessness, are realistic at that time. To allay such anxiety and fear, the developing individual comes to learn a set of rules of operation and varying adaptive techniques which assure survival by warding off the threat of either punishment or the loss of love from significant people in the child's life.

During the course of the infant's learning to adjust to the expanding world about him, anxiety comes to have a very useful purpose as a reaction to something perceived, consciously or unconsciously, as a threat to the established sets of behavior the individual has developed. Such "signal anxiety" alerts the individual to initiate action which prevents his mode of operation from being disrupted. This type of anxiety, within limits, is useful, since it serves as a constant scanning mechanism which perceives threatening situations with a great sensitivity and in turn leads the individual to take adaptive action.

The nature of early childhood relationships may serve unduly to perpetuate feelings of anxiety and helplessness. When support and security are not sufficient to allay the child's normal developing sense of insecurity and helplessness, misperceptions occur which may lead to the distortion of all later relationships. Early fears of disapproval may be transferred from significant individuals upon whom the child is dependent for security to their representatives in later life. Such distortion, as an expression of anxiety, gives rise to further anxiety.

Individuals who later develop "anxiety reactions" or "anxiety states" appear to have a pattern of response for handling anxiety which does not necessitate gross distortion of reality; i.e., repression comes to serve as the predominant technique in the individual's defensive strategy. Massive use of repression is most readily perpetuated in an atmosphere which discourages communication about things related to sex or aggression and where the implicit assumption is that "certain things are not to be talked about." In all families there are parental and cultural taboos about certain topics and ideas. The child learns by trial and error that some things are not to be discussed and that it is better if one does not "even think such things." For example, a little girl, first expressing the wish that she is going to marry Daddy when she grows up, will normally find this idea laughed at and ridiculed, and she will soon come to inhibit any expression of such wishes. In time, she will not even "think" such things. The range of ideas that are acceptable thus soon becomes defined for the child.

In certain families, however, the repressive influences reach excessive proportions. Inquiry and reflection are discouraged. Introspection or self-examination are simply not considered appropriate. Disruptive stimuli are to be ignored or avoided. Intellectualizing and the active seeking of information are inhibited. The implicit philosophy is "What you don't know can't hurt you," and entertaining an unacceptable thought is the equivalent of committing the deed.

SUMMARY

The following assumptions are helpful in understanding an anxiety reaction:

1. Anxiety is an exceedingly uncomfortable, often intolerable, state, implicit in which are extreme feelings of helplessness.

2. Anxiety reactions are precipitated by a present situation which serves to reactivate earlier fears and conflicts. While the reaction may appear to be "irrational" in terms of the apparently benign factors that precipitate it, the threat which is symbolically represented is one that originally involved devastating consequences: loss of love, physical punishment, and (ultimately) death.

3. The major defense operating in individuals prone to anxiety attacks is *repression*. Although repression is a defense used by everyone to some extent, it leaves the individual extremely uncritical in his thinking, immature, and unreflective when it constitutes the predominant aspect of his defensive strategy.

4. Anxiety, perhaps more than any other emotion, directly in-

volves physiological reactions which may be mistaken for organic disease.

MANAGEMENT

Many people who visit physicians complain of bodily symptoms which are nothing more or less than anxiety reactions. Numerous factors determine the perpetuation of these anxiety states, not the least of which may be the doctor's reaction to the presented bodily complaints. The physician serves these patients by gratifying their dependency needs when they are described in terms of bodily complaints. Once such a relationship has been established, it is extremely difficult to refocus the patient's attention from his bodily sensations to the issues underlying his anxiety.

The physician must use extreme care when inquiring into the nature of a patient's complaints to determine the underlying cause. The physical manifestations of anxiety, such as the rapid heart, nausea, vomiting, diarrhea, sweating, and flushing, are frequently accepted by both the patient and the doctor as evidence of organic illness. These are the classical manifestations of anxiety that can easily be misinterpreted by the physician as signs of physical ill-health, particularly when the patient relates his symptoms without also describing the feelings of anxiety which accompany this condition. The patient often omits describing these feelings to defend himself against a loss of self-esteem in the process; *anxiety, for many people, is not a respectable illness.* In view of this, the physician should exercise a great deal of caution while acquiring the medical history of the patient and questioning the kinds of situations that appear to precipitate the symptoms reported. He must inquire into all areas of experience, past and present, to determine some of the elements that add to the discomfort of the anxious patient.

An anxiety attack is a disorder in which successful treatment can be easily achieved; conversely, it is one in which the patient's distress is easily reinforced. The physician quite often unwittingly perpetuates the patient's difficulty by behaving as if he concurs with the patient that it is a physical illness. For example, the physician is himself anxious to do something to alleviate the patient's suffering. Knowing that many readily available barbiturates or tranquilizers are useful for easing anxiety, he may prescribe these drugs without explaining their purpose. Thinking that the patient is a "neurotic" and that "suggestion works well with all neurotics," he conveys the impression that the drug is a panacea. The patient then concludes that there is something physically wrong with him since drugs presumably are not prescribed except for physical illnesses. Even when given an explanation for the drug, many patients will still misinterpret such medication. If no explanation is made, the physician will have only fostered the patient's notion that he has a physical illness. Because of the cultural unacceptability of emotional illness, most patients are quite acquiescent in letting the physician perpetuate this view.

One of the techniques that can be employed in the treatment of anxiety-ridden patients is *environmental manipulation*. The environment can sometimes be modified so as to remove some of the dangers in the situation. As an illustration, an individual who grew up in fear of a sadistic, cruel father, whom he could never please, finds himself in a job situation where the foreman is unconsciously perceived as the father. He would need either long-term psychotherapy to get over the unconscious feelings he has about his father, or he would have to change his job and find another type of foreman. The latter may be the more feasible and sensible action. The patient might get along fairly well with such a change, provided the new foreman is a kindly, sympathetic, helpful person who does not threaten the patient's sense of autonomy.

Thus, certain kinds of environmental manipulation quite frequently can make life tolerable for the anxiety-prone patient. They do not make the patient a different person; he is still as vulnerable to the type of anxiety experienced before the environmental change and is quite likely to have recurring attacks upon meeting situations similar to those that threatened him prior to the change.

Another solution to the hypothetical problem cited above would be to interview the patient's wife, who basically may be a kind person with a great deal of strength and genuine regard for her husband's welfare, but who may not really understand the anxiety situation. If the situation were explained to her and she were advised to be more sympathetic and supportive toward her husband who has no control over his symptoms, life for the patient might prove more tolerable. The support from the wife in such a situation would strengthen the patient's defenses. This is the type of environmental manipulation which, in psychiatric prescription parlance, would set "mother" (wife) against "father" (the boss), thereby obtaining a kind of protector for the "little child" (patient) who is misinterpreting his environment. Such a supportive maneuver may make the patient quite comfortable without extensive treatment.

Another method for treating anxiety reactions is the *educative technique,* which is to teach the patient to understand the real nature of his difficulties. Initially, this technique is not very satisfactory to the patient, because he would prefer to believe his difficulties are physical; but if he can be made to go along with it, he may be able to achieve much greater comfort. The physiological effects of anxiety, as well as the interplay between the emotions and bodily sensations, should be explained to the patient. Fifteen-minute sessions over a period of time (six months) of this type of educative technique can produce beneficial results in many cases.

Many of the physiological symptoms of anxiety attacks result from hyperventilation (overbreathing), which may be so slight that it is not apparent to the patient. Sometimes it may occur after a disturbing dream (which may be immediately repressed). The *hyperventilation syndrome* includes feelings of lightheadedness, faintness, profuse perspiration, shortness of breath, pain in the head or heart region, and tingling sensations in the extremities. In extreme cases, loss of consciousness or convulsions may occur. It is often helpful to demonstrate to the patient that these symptoms can be consciously produced by having him overbreathe for a period of two to three minutes in a sitting position. It is also worthwhile to explain the physiological mechanism behind the biochemical changes which lead to the respiratory alkalosis of which the symptoms are pathognomic. In many cases, this will immediately relieve the patient of the misconceptions that he has "heart trouble" or some physical disorder of which he has not been told. It also prepares the way for further investigation of the causes that lead to the overbreathing.

In the practice of medicine today, the physician's responsibility to his patient goes further than the determination of whether a disorder is "functional" or "organic." It is the physician's responsibility in a functional disturbance to assist the patient to learn and understand the cause. It is a recognized fact that human beings possess a tremendous ability for self-cure when they are apprised of the reasons for their particular illness. Many intestinal disturbances are of psychic orign, for example, but if this is not explained to the patient, he will continue to think that he has a physically caused intestinal disturbance.

When undertaking the treatment of an anxiety reaction with physical manifestations of illness, the doctor must be prepared for the patient's dependency upon him. If the physician can understand and accept this, he has a good possibility of achieving beneficial results for the patient when employing the educative technique. When the physician has been successful in educating the patient to the point where he perceives the reasons for his illness, it then becomes the patient's responsibility to change his reaction to the environmental situation. This may be a lengthy process, and the patient's dependency on the physician may prove irksome; but perseverance and patience on the part of the physician in many cases will produce results which more than compensate for the effort.

In the treatment of the anxious patient, the most important point is to *deflect the patient's thinking from the organic symptoms of his illness* and to educate him to perceive and accept that his symptoms are basically related to anxiety. Otherwise, if the patient is permitted to go on thinking that his anxiety is a physical disease, he will go from doctor to doctor complaining about his physical symptoms and over a period of years will have obtained symptomatic treatments without end.

4

Phobias and

Phobic Reactions

Closely allied to anxiety states are those reactions of fear which are called *phobias*.

Phobia: *a persistent fear attached to an object or situation which is objectively not a source of danger. The phobic person usually regards his fears as inexplicable yet experiences overpowering anxiety when confronted with the phobic situation.*

In phobic reactions, the usual physiological reactions to anxiety often appear: perspiration, tremor, rapid breathing, diarrhea, vomiting, "tightness in the chest," rapid heart and pulse rate.

Theoretically, any situation or object may become the focus of a phobia. Common phobic foci include heights, closed spaces, subways, elevators, dirt, germs, open spaces, water, crowds, strangers, animals, and the dark.

CLASSIFICATION

NORMAL FEARS VS. PHOBIAS

Although in theory it may be difficult to differentiate fears based on realistic dangers from truly phobic reactions, in actual practice the patient's response to the perceived danger usually clearly indicates whether his fear is rational or whether it is serving such purposes as those discussed under "Psychodynamics." Thus, to evaluate a fear of flying, one does not need to become involved in the statistics of airplane accidents. While there are many objects and situations that most people variably dislike or fear to some extent (snakes, death, heights), the phobic patient will himself usually recognize the irrational intensity and inappropriateness of his feelings.

PHOBIAS VS. PHOBIC REACTIONS

Phobias (irrational fears) may be present in any number of disorders, ranging from the neurotic to the psychotic. In the disorder labeled "phobic reaction," the phobia is the primary and basic symptom, without evidences of other predominant psychopathy. The phobic reaction is thus a neurotic classification and is closely allied in psychogenesis to those other neurotic disorders labeled "anxiety state" and "conversion hysteria."

PSYCHODYNAMICS

The beginning of a phobia is usually an acute anxiety attack, indicating that some threatening impulse or feeling has been triggered by the environment. Because anxiety, like fear, precipitates essentially a "fight or flight" reaction resulting from the intolerable feelings that accompany it, the human organism attempts to develop defenses to protect itself. The first line of defense is invariably *repression*, but his defense may fail to keep the threat sufficiently from conscious awareness or the anxiety within tolerable limits. *Displacement* (allied with repression) may then be utilized, a defense which leads to the development of a phobia.

Displacement: *the process by which an emotion or feeling is unconsciously transferred from its source or object to a more acceptable substitute.*

Utilizing displacement, the individual combats his diffuse anxiety by binding it to a particular object or situation which can then be avoided. In many instances, life is thus made tolerable for the individual. The specificity of the fear makes it manageable. However confining or restricting the phobia may become in terms of life's experiences or opportunities, the patient has at least arrived at a solution which offers some escape from the intolerable effects of prolonged diffuse anxiety.

How is the phobic object selected? The specific choice of a phobic object is generally fully understood only through intensive study of the patient's past history. Although universally symbolic meanings for the common phobic objects have been suggested, these are not invariably valid. Elongated objects may symbolize the phallus, and enclosed areas may symbolize the womb; but, like other objects and situations, they may have many other meanings. A fear of the street, for example, may symbolize fears of leaving home, sexual temptation, exhibitionistic impulses, being attacked, etc.

The choice of some phobic objects can be explained partially in terms of *contiguity* and *continuity*. For example:

A woman walking in the street experiences an acute panic about an impulse pertaining to unacceptable homosexual wishes. The fear may be displaced or pushed out of awareness by attaching the anxiety to some circumstances in the immediate environment, i.e., the street.

A patient had a sudden impulse that she was going to take a kitchen knife and stab her three-year-old child who was causing her concern and anxiety. At that time a whistle on a passing railroad train sounded. The patient became phobic about locomotive whistles.

The choice of the phobic object sometimes appears to be explained by simple determinants of present association, as in the examples above, but these determinants frequently explain only the situation precipitating the phobia without fully explaining the total condensation involved in the selection of the particular object. Clarification of the complex reasons for the choice of the specific phobic object usually necessitates, through prolonged investigation, the recall of childhood experiences for which the phobic adult has long been amnesic. Multiple phobias may develop, each with its own equation.

Phobic persons frequently develop phobic companions, such as a husband or a child, who stand by continuously to prevent them from experiencing acute panic or anxiety. Such companions may become very dedicated people, often finding secondary gain for themselves by becoming "collaborators" in a mutually reinforcing cycle.

A merchant with a very fine store in a profitable business area had a wife who became phobic. He gave up his business, devoting all of his time to being with her. She would not let him outside her view. If he walked the dog, she stood at the window to watch him, so that he would not go beyond her vision. Apart from financial difficulties because of his being unable to work, he did not appear greatly concerned by this state of affairs and, in fact, seemed to take great satisfaction in being needed by his wife. It was not until he was called upon to leave the city to visit his sick mother that he expressed dissatisfaction with the conflicting demands made on him.

There is an unconscious wish in persons with phobias to be taken care of and to have their dependency needs satisfied. They may use their companion as a *symbolic parent*, i.e., as a "good mother," who will protect them from their fears. They may also use the companion as a "bad mother"; in keeping the companion with them, they are reassured that their aggressive impulse will not be acted upon or thought about. Some phobic patients keep a companion to protect themselves from acting out other forbidden impulses, as if the companion lessened the necessity of watching over their own impulses. In a sense, this maneuver is based on the feeling that "You can't lose control if there is somebody present who will manage you." Phobias can be used aggressively to control others and gain special privileges. There are some cases reported in which the need for a companion is motivated by the desire to disengage the companion from some other relationship which the phobic person resents. A phobic girl, for example, by requiring her mother to be constantly at her side, assures herself that her mother and father cannot be alone together. A situation which guarantees exclusive possession is thus created. In most instances, the relationship between patient and companion is one of *mutual intimidation and satisfaction*.

If a phobia is successful, the phobic object will hold the anxiety within tolerable limits. If the phobic person has a recurrence of the original anxiety, stimulated by some situation in the immediate environment, the phobia may then have to be extended.

> A woman had a subway phobia which began with an inability to ride an express train between two fairly distant locations. Gradually, it developed that she would have to get off the train at each express stop and then get back on the train before it started again. Later, she had to get off at each local stop. It eventually developed that she would have to get off at each stop, wait until her anxiety diminished, get on the next train, and get off again at the next stop until her destination was reached.

Phobias are sometimes extremely disabling. Some persons who have phobias in a severe form cannot leave their apartment or home. They frequently cannot cross the threshold of a certain room. They feel helpless and are often unable to work or move about. One might say, "This is silly; take the patient by the arm and tell him, 'Let's go.'" When the phobic situation is transgressed by such force, however, the transgression precipitates an acute panic reaction which is very painful to the patient. The phobic patient then feels disabled, often completely losing the ability to work and the freedom to move about.

Children with phobias often have the same kinds of fears as adults. The nature of the feared situation may be of less significance than is the anxiety of the child to face the situation alone. The so-called "school phobia," for example, is usually much less a fear of school than anxiety over being separated from the mother. Frequently the mother herself has phobias or has fear about having the child away from her, a fact that is communicated to the child in subtle or sometimes obvious ways.

Children tend to outgrow phobias as their capacity to master difficulties increases; those who do not outgrow them become candidates for the common adult phobic syndrome. The most common childhood phobias are: fear of being alone, fear of the dark, and fear of animals. Fear of being alone may symbolize a fear of independence, or attack, or of loss of control of forbidden impulses, or a fear of loss of love and dependency gratifications. Fear of the dark is usually directly related to the fear of being alone. The fear of animals frequently reflects a distorted representation of unconscious perceptions of human beings:

> The classic case of Freud on phobias was that of "Little Hans" ("Analysis of a Phobia in a Five-Year-Old Boy"), a boy who refused to go into the street for fear that a horse would bite him. Analysis revealed an exceedingly complex structure behind this phobia, basic to which was an intense fear of punishment stemming from unconscious hostility toward the father and a competition with the father for the mother's attentions which were fused with sexual meanings. By displacing his fear from his father to the horse, he could both love his father and avoid the object of his phobia.[1]

---

[1] As indicated on page 28, the traditional interpretations of anxiety, phobic, and hysterical reactions stress the role of unacceptable sexual (oedipal) impulses, with fear of punishment (castration) as the result. In the case of Little Hans, the child was indeed very preoccupied with sexual differences between him and his parents and had noticed the large penis on the horse he had seen. However, authorities who believe that the primal source of all anxiety is the separation from the mother would emphasize the dependency aspects and assume that the mother-child relationship must have been disrupted prior to the emergence of the boy's sexual preoccupation for the total sequence to have occurred. In this regard, it is significant that it was the mother who first threatened Little Hans with castration when she found him touching his penis at age three-and-a-half. His relationship with his mother had also been jeopardized by the arrival of a baby sister. The strong motivations for dependency gratifications found in patients with phobic reactions strongly militate against the adequacy of any theory which solely emphasizes the sexual aspect of a phobia.

PSYCHOGENESIS

There are several common elements in the experience or personality development of those who develop phobias:

EARLY FAILURES AT MASTERY

The person who develops phobias has generally not succeeded in the mastery of early childhood problems. There are many possible reasons for this failure:

1. Parental intimidation often keeps a child from mastering any situation, whether it is related to sex, aggression, or assertiveness.

2. Parents may fail to support children at the appropriate time, subjecting them to derision, ridicule, and humiliation. Siblings may also contribute to this belittlement.

3. The child may simply copy or emulate a very phobic, timid parent who communicates phobic attitudes to the child.

4. Some persons may have organic difficulties which make them less able to master life situations, e.g., the mentally defective child may often be phobic.

Every child, in the course of development, has to learn a method of dealing with impulses of sex, aggression, and self-assertion. The anxiety accompanying these impulses may lead to a guilt-filled, fearful child who specifically fears parental retaliation. If he performs a forbidden act, expectations of punishment may result, guilt feelings arise, and self-esteem and self-confidence may be diminished. In such a setting, anxiety no longer serves the adaptive function of instigating patterns of assertion which lead to mastery.

EARLY WITHDRAWAL PATTERNS

In an activity or social situation that is filled with anxiety or fear, the child who becomes phobic either then or later in life may withdraw rather than learn techniques for dealing with the situation. In the adult who had the developmental history of a phobic personality, one frequently finds the report of multiple childhood phobias: fear of the dark, of snakes, of swimming, of animals, or of being hurt. Such patterns are easily reactivated when difficult hurdles must be faced in later life.

REPRESSIVE INFLUENCES

As found with anxiety reactions, the patient's past history frequently reveals a setting in which communication about sex and aggression has been inhibited, and in which repression has become a prominent defense. In our culture which can be quite open in relation to hostile and sexual stimuli, it is difficult for massive repression to work indefinitely. When defensive failures occur, other defenses, including displacement, are then called into action.

PROJECTION

Related perhaps to these repressive influences is the tendency toward a view of reality in which the world is distorted in terms of inner impulses and needs. The implicit assumption is that "It can't be in me; it is out there." The degree to which responsibility can be transferred (projected) to outside causes can come very close to a more pathological defense (projection), which will be discussed later.[2]

SUMMARY

The following assumptions are helpful in understanding a phobic reaction:

1. Phobic reactions are closely allied to anxiety reactions and often elicit similar physiological responses.
2. By the mechanism of displacement, the phobic person has

---

[2] Because of the degree of similarity represented, it is sometimes difficult to differentiate phobic from paranoid features, a distinction which has important implications for treatment and prognosis.

arrived at a solution which offers some escape from the intolerable effects of prolonged diffuse anxiety, since the specificity of the fear now makes it manageable.

3. Among other purposes, the phobia generally serves the purpose of satisfying strong dependency needs, eliciting care, attention, and companionship.

4. The disorder labeled "phobic reaction" is in the neurotic classification, since the phobia is the primary and basic symptom without other predominant psychopathy. A phobia can occur in other settings, however, appearing with other psychopathy and, in some instances, serving to mask more serious (psychotic) disorders.

MANAGEMENT

Several techniques exist for treating phobias, many similar to those used in relieving anxiety. Some authorities believe that the original repressed impulse should be uncovered, thereby leading to an understanding of the original trauma. This can be accomplished only through *long-term psychotherapy*.

Another kind of treatment involves the direct use of *suggestion:*

Some doctors issue "safety passes" which are carried by the patient to "assure" him safe passage.

Knowing that alcohol relieves their phobic feelings, some patients carry miniature bottles of whiskey. Although it may never be used, it serves as a symbol that they really are not helpless since they can always take immediate recourse to alcohol.

Hypnosis has been used to relieve the intensity of a phobia. Best results are generally obtained when the suggestion has been given in stages rather than when removal of the phobia has been attempted precipitously with one suggestion.

Other unusual approaches utilizing suggestion may also work. For example, a phobic patient who was afraid that he would die if he left his home was bet $1,000 by his physician that this would not occur. This wager resulted in the patient's leaving his home for the first time in over three months.

Phobic patients may be extremely suggestible, naive, and unreflective. They often uncritically accept procedures that are not thoroughly rational and that border on the "magical." The man who was bet that he would not die, for example, appeared to have no awareness of the ludicrous arrangement in which, even if he "won" the bet, he would not be able to collect.

Drugs can also be used, since they sometimes diminish the anxiety and thus eliminate the need for displacement.

A combination of some understanding of the psychodynamics of the particular situation with an understanding of the early fearful situations in childhood is most helpful. This task is made easier if there has been a phobic parent whose phobic pattern can be distinguished from that of the patient. The phobic companion can be very useful in treating the phobic patient because he has extraordinary power over the patient and is endowed with attributes which border on the magical. Although it is not wise to divorce the phobic companion precipitously from the phobic patient, it is often possible to show the patient how he is using the other person in a destructive and hostile fashion. It is helpful if the patient can come to understand the psychodynamics of his early childhood phobia and his wish to be taken care of. Since a great deal of secondary gain accrues to the phobic person in terms of care, attention, and support, it is often necessary to reduce such rewards. Such a rational approach works with many phobic patients. It is probably best to reduce the "magic" in the situation to a minimum, letting the patient recognize that there is no magical cure and that overprotection, love, and support will not allow him to master situations if he always looks to another person for help.

5

Bodily Expressions
of Psychological Difficulties

As the mediator between the external environment and the self as a psychological entity, the body may become the focus of functional disturbances in which psychological difficulties are expressed primarily physiologically. Since there may be a striking difference between the patient's ideas about what is happening to his body and the doctor's concept of what is actually going on, these difficulties are often the most frustrating and difficult for the physician to handle effectively.

CLASSIFICATION

Classification of the physiological complaints and symptoms which express psychological difficulties involves distinctions which cut across both psychogenesis and psychodynamics.

CONVERSION REACTIONS

Conversion reactions are bodily symptoms without ascertainable physiological basis which appear to arise as a symbolic resolution (conversion) of emotional conflicts. A stiff arm, for example, may symbolize an erection; hysterical blindness may symbolize an unwillingness to "see" some unacceptable aspect of reality. Conversion symptoms serve to diminish consciously felt anxiety about an actual conflict which is repressed from awareness. These symptoms are usually in parts of the body which are mainly under voluntary control and are of three main types:

1. Altered sensation (anesthesia, hyperesthesia, and paresthesia)
2. Loss of motor function (paralysis, paraplegia, aphonia)
3. Involuntary movement (tics, tremors, seizures)

A conversion symptom may imitate a physiological disorder observed in someone else. It generally conforms to the layman's conception of bodily functioning; for example, the typical "stocking" or "glove" anesthesia ending evenly around an extremity rather than conforming to the actual anatomical distribution of motor and sensory nerves. "Secondary gain" is often conspicuous, as the symptom serves to manipulate the patient's present life situation. Frequently the patient seems unconcerned ("la belle indifférence") about his impaired function. Although presumably typical of a conversion reaction, this attitude is not invariably present.

Conversion reactions often have a sudden or dramatic onset. Traditionally considered in the category of a neurotic disorder labeled "hysteria," conversion reactions may occur in the psychoses. Likewise, they may occur in personalities other than those descriptively labeled "hysterical personalities," namely, egocentric, labile, histrionic, sexually provocative individuals who rely on repression as a major defense. Although traditionally conceived as a defense against sexual and oedipal impulses, the conversion reaction, like anxiety and phobic reactions, invariably also involves strong dependency and hostile feelings. Characteristic of those who develop conversion reactions is early affectional deprivation resulting in an immature and dependent personality and the playing of the "baby" role in the family context.

PSYCHOPHYSIOLOGICAL DISORDERS

Psychophysiological disorders refer to bodily symptoms which are due to the chronic exaggeration of a normal physiological expression of emotion. The long-continued visceral expression of an emotion eventually leads to structural changes. A physiological basis (rather than a symbolic one, as in a conversion reaction) for the origin of symptoms is thus formed. Although organs and viscera innervated by the autonomic nervous system are typically involved, the expanding list of so-called "psychosomatic" disorders now includes those in which the mediating role of the autonomic nervous system is not clearly established. Disorders sometimes classified in this category include: the neurodermatoses, psoriasis, atopic dermatitis, bronchial asthma, paroxysmal tachycardia, peptic ulcer, constipation, ulcerative and mucous colitis, migraine, hypertension, and arthritis. It must be stressed that the emotional components in each of these disorders varies greatly with different patients and that they cannot be considered the only significant causative influence. The specificity of "choice" of the symptom has been attributed to a variety of factors, including the particular personality characteristics of the patient, the particular type of conflict the patient is experiencing, the predominant type of emotion being experienced, and organic weakness which makes a particular organ vulnerable to specific or nonspecific stress. Most authorities would allow for the possibility of a physical vulnerability of the particular organ involved. Nevertheless, emotional antecedents, particularly related to the control of hostility, are often striking in the precipitation and exacerbation of these disorders.

HYPOCHONDRIASIS

Hypochondriasis refers to a persistent pathological concern about the health of the body, expressed in marked diffuse preoccupation about the function of many organs. This preoccupation tends to usurp all other interests. Although at one time the term "hypochondriacal" was used only for those patients who had no organic pathology, it is used now sometimes for those who have excessive preoccupation with actual organic illness. Symptoms of the hypochondriacal state include complaints of pressure in the head, poor memory, inability to concentrate, irritability, poor sleep patterns, which accompany multiple aches and pains—all described compulsively and repeatedly by the patient. Hypochondriasis is a compensation for serious defects in self-esteem or for unaccomplished ideals in life. Although typically classified as a neurotic disorder, hypochondriasis may actually incorporate beliefs about the body which are delusional and hence psychotic.

OTHER BODY-IMAGE DISTURBANCES

"Body-image" or "body concept" refers to the ways in which one experiences and evaluates one's body. Sensory perceptions from skeletal musculature, surface of the body, as well as sensory perceptions from inside the body—all contribute to the "body concept." This involves the degree of clarity or distortion in perception of the body, the degree of satisfaction or dissatisfaction felt about the body, and the nature of the total relationship between the person and his body as an object. Body-image disturbances subsume a wide variety of clinical disorders which are not etiologically related, although they have in common the fact that the major symptom is related to how the body is experienced by the patient. The following phenomena would be examples of disturbances typically referred to as disturbances in body-image:

In some cases of *brain damage*, patients may give very distorted descriptions of paralyzed body parts, or deny the existence of certain body parts, or deny the existence of their paralysis.

In the phenomenon of *phantom limb*, the patient may continue to experience a removed limb, often with pain, as if the limb were still physically present.

In *functional disorders*, some patients will invest an abnormally great interest in the body and its parts which may be expressed as dissatisfaction with minor or nonexistent "defects" in the external appearance of the body. It may also be expressed in abnormal concern with the health and integrity of the body and its functioning (hypochondriasis).

Certain body parts may be invested with sexual or symbolic meaning. Some persons seek to change their bodily appearance or facial features for reasons of extreme unconscious conflict which have little to do with their actual appearance. In one patient, for example, a certain physical feature may symbolically represent a relationship to a relative whose way of life is not condoned. Another feature may be unconsciously viewed as revealing hidden truths about the person. As the nose may reveal the fact that one is of a certain nationality or that one has been drinking, unconsciously it may be perceived also as revealing other truths, particularly unacceptable ones. Because the nose also has symbolic likeness to the sexual organs (placement in center of body, an opening with a discharge), it may also become the focus of anxiety and concern actually displaced from the genitals. Such unconscious conflicts may necessitate that any surgery on the part will be judged unsatisfactory by the patient.

Distortions in the perception of normal body functions may also occur, e.g., normal sensations or noises in the stomach may be misinterpreted as indications of pregnancy or cancer, misinterpretations which sometimes persist in spite of physicians' reassurances to the contrary.

Delusional ideas (false beliefs not amenable to correction by the weight of external evidence) sometimes center about the body. In a psychotic depression, for example, the patient frequently feels that his body is dead or that it is rotting away. Anorexia nervosa patients may perceive their bodies as normal and "just right" even when they are reduced to emaciated figures.

PSYCHOGENESIS [1]

The role which the body comes to play as mediator between the external environment and the self as a psychological entity is the

---

[1] In some instances, it appears feasible to discuss psychogenesis prior to psychodynamics.

result of numerous influences, both physical and psychological. It is important to recognize that a child is not born with an awareness or understanding of where his body ends and the world or external reality begins. One can observe the joy of a young child as he learns that some part of his body, such as his hand, has a special relationship to him and that the movement of a finger or of the hand itself is related to some kind of control by him. The frustration over things that are not like this, such as the mother's breast, can also be readily observed.

The distinction between self and nonself is sometimes referred to as *body boundaries* or *ego boundaries*. If the normal process of learning this distinction becomes disrupted,[2] the basis on which the distinction actually rests never becomes firmly established in the child's bodily experience. This state may persist through adulthood, leaving the person vulnerable to the development of disorders involving faulty perception of both self and external reality.

In the course of the growing child's contact with reality, sensory impressions are continually conveyed by means of the kinesthetic, visual, and the tactile systems, and lead to a highly differentiated form of bodily awareness. Important values, real and symbolic, come to be placed on the body and its parts. These values are derived from general cultural influences as well as from specific experiences in the family.

Early patterns of family and cultural communication about the body and the role of the body vary greatly:

Studies have indicated the tremendous differences by which families communicate the values they place upon the child's body and upon such concepts as "sickness" and "health." In some families, for example, a rise of one degree of temperature in the child is cause for alarm and panic; in others, serious illness goes unnoticed. If attention, acceptance, service, comfort, reassurance, and love become associated too exclusively with being ill, patterns of illness may be

---

[2] Conditions which may disrupt this process of learning include: excessive infantile gratifications which discourage learning, constitutional or physical disturbances which limit learning, or excessive frustration or deprivation experienced in the process of learning.

reinforced which are perpetuated throughout life. If illness is generally ignored, a pattern of denial of illness may be formed.

Sickness and health are often consciously or unconsciously equated with "sin" and "virtue," respectively. Physical illness may be interpreted as punishment for one's sins or moral transgressions. Physical health, on the other hand, may be perceived as the reward for being virtuous. Thus, one presumably "deserves" what one gets; one also "gets" what one really deserves. Unconscious guilt may thus lead to an anticipation of punishment in terms of bodily harm. Religious beliefs and practices may reinforce such conceptions of physical health, infusing them with values which have little to do with the actual physical state of the body.

His state of handsomeness or ugliness, adequacy or inadequacy, and strength or weakness, as well as familial and cultural attitudes about these states, are conveyed to a child at an early age through numerous family interactions. These evaluations are often enduring, even long after they are no longer based on reality. Thus, a person who was obese as a child may continue to perceive himself as being overweight even when he is of normal bodily size. The "ugly duckling" child may develop attitudes of self-derogation which persist long after she has become a "swan."

Pain or the denial of pain may result in varied responses in different families and may express "messages" which have little to do with the physical problem involved. Expressions of pain quickly become interpersonal phenomena. Pain may serve a self-excusing function, for example, by relieving the person of certain responsibilities. "Bearing" pain may be interpreted as a testimonial to one's bravery and physical strength, to one's moral fiber and character, or to one's relationship with the deity. Pain is seldom a purely physiological reaction without psychological components.

Quite different attitudes may be conveyed about the worth, cleanliness, or acceptability of the body and bodily functions. In our culture, for example, anal functions are frequently fused with shame and guilt. Although there may be some intrinsic wisdom in many of these attitudes, it nevertheless seems that our culture sometimes perpetuates many irrational attitudes about normal bodily functions.

Genital differences between boys and girls may be associated with attitudes of damage and inferiority. Some women, for example, have unconscious resentment toward men because being a woman is interpreted as having been deprived of something which the man has. Attitudes of self-damage may stem from unwarranted earlier beliefs about the effects of masturbation. Threats to the child that masturbation leads one to "lose his mind," that it will "cause the penis to fall off," or that it prevents one from becoming a "man" are all common in our culture. Attitudes of damage and inferiority, established at an early age, may be perpetuated and serve as a source of difficulty in relating intimately to the opposite sex.

Different cultures place quite different values on certain bodily characteristics, such as thinness, light skin color, height, curl of the hair, etc. Our culture places great value on everlasting youth and beauty, an ideal which is presumably within everybody's reach if one only utilizes available beauty aids.

Attitudes of excessive modesty or immodesty about the body vary greatly, stemming partly from how parents have responded to the child's normal exhibitionistic impulses which reach a peak around the age of two or three years. Exposure of the body even in the course of a physical examination may be a source of great embarrassment and anxiety to certain patients.

Thus, under the influences of particular experiences in a particular culture, the growing individual comes ultimately to develop a conception and perception of his body which often directly mirrors his total adaptive and integrative capacities and which may determine his reaction to both imagined and real physical disturbances.

PSYCHODYNAMICS

The influences that motivate particular bodily expressions of psychological difficulties have already been suggested in the preceding discussion. Vulnerabilities established by early life experiences may not become apparent, however, until precipitated by present specific or nonspecific stress. In some instances, this stress will be evoked by a change that is occurring in the body itself. Such a change may occur as a result of normal aging, particularly at the time of adolescence or late adulthood. It may also occur because of sickness, particularly as a result of physical trauma. At such times, earlier attitudes and misperceptions may be reactivated and precipitate severe psychological disturbances.

During pubescence and adolescence, there is much concern about the appearance of acne, the deepening of the voice, the growth of axillary and pubic hair, the size of the breasts, and the size and new sensations in the penis and testicles. Bodily changes at this time sometimes produce a sense of loss of the earlier image; these changes also arouse anxiety in that they imply that the adolescent is now becoming a peer of his parent. The effects of these changes in other people are often either anticipated or dreaded by the adolescent. On some occasions, his anxiety is aroused because the expected changes are not occurring or are not occurring in a desired time or way.

In a later period of life, the "middle-age spread," balding, and observable skin changes may have a profound effect on the image of masculinity or femininity the person holds about himself or herself. People who have been excessively interested in the appearance of their bodies may then become preoccupied with the functioning of their bodies. This may be translated into concern about illness, leading to hypochondriacal concerns.

In other instances, changes in the person's body as a result of surgery may force a shift in the person's self-perception which disrupts the integrity of the body-image. It is thus not uncommon for plastic surgeons to find that, although cosmetic surgery may be extremely successful from their own point of view, certain patients continue to express dissatisfaction with the result. The change may result in a "loss reaction" and elicit feelings of depression. Surgical results may also amplify into consciousness the unconscious conflict motivating the desire for change and thus produce anxiety.

Sudden changes in the body may also occur as a result of accidents or surgical trauma. In persons who have had amputations, the perception of the lost part of the body normally remains for some time, as if the part were still present. The sensations are such that during the postoperative phase following a leg amputation, some of these patients will get out of bed and fall on the side of the absent leg because they have the feeling that the leg is still there. Immediately following the operation, the phantom is usually perceived where the real limb was; during recovery, this phantom gradually shrinks until the total loss is fully integrated into the individual's body-image.

As opposed to those instances in which the precipitating stress stems from changes that occur to the body itself, this stress may also be related to emotional conflicts arising from present interpersonal relationships. Anxiety, hostility, or frustrated dependency needs may lead to bodily expressions like those that occurred at some significant period in childhood and that elicited love and attention. If these emotions become chronic, they may give rise to those disorders classified as "psychosomatic," although physiological vulnerabilities may also play their part in these disorders.

Physical symptoms may serve to produce immediate satisfactions which tend to perpetuate the symptoms in some patients. They may, for example, serve to obtain love and affection from a needed companion. The exacerbation of hypochondriacal symptoms, for example, tends to occur and recur at the time of a real or fantasied loss. Frequently the patient has had a close attachment with the mother or a mother-surrogate who was overly concerned about bodily functions. When this person's attention is turned away from the patient to some other person, the patient may grow resentful and physical symptoms may ensue. Illness may also help perpetuate a dependency on another person. If one is sick, one can get help through an attachment to a doctor or to a relative because of the illness. Somatic complaints may allow release by giving vent to aggressive feelings. A wife in menopause, for instance, may become sick and come to the point of hypochondriacal preoccupation with her symptoms as a way of enlisting a great deal of activity and interest on the part of her husband, thus preventing him from "running around."

SUMMARY

The following assumptions are helpful in understanding bodily expressions of psychological difficulties:

1. The body is an extremely personal organ of communication. As the mediator between the environment and the self as a psychological entity, it may become the focus of numerous disturbances in which psychological difficulties are expressed physiologically.

2. These difficulties may be expressed through symbolic resolution of emotional conflicts (conversion reactions), through structural changes occurring on the basis of chronic exaggeration of a normal physiological expression of emotion ("psychosomatic" disorders), through excessive preoccupation with the function of the body (hypochondriasis), or through numerous other body-image disturbances.

3. The individual's total adaptive and integrative capacities are mirrored in these difficulties and determine his reaction to both imagined and real physical disturbances.

MANAGEMENT

CONVERSION REACTIONS

Conversion reactions may present a difficult diagnostic problem, involving the differentiation of functional and organic etiology. Since the symptoms of conversion reactions may mimic those actually occurring with organic disease, the full armamentarium of medical diagnostic techniques must often be utilized. Psychological tests are also helpful in determining the role of emotional factors. Patients with conversion reactions are often highly suggestible and may respond to "magical" procedures. To remove the symptom in such a way that the patient "saves face," without embarrassment and through understanding of the need for and the cause of the symptom, is a good method. Frequently the symptom will disappear when it has served its purpose through the secondary gain it elicits. Patients with conversion reactions are often extremely frustrating since their use of repression and suppression is extensive. One may often be in doubt as to whether the patient on occasion is deliberately distorting the truth. Although conversion reactions were at one time believed to have an excellent prognosis in psychotherapy, the accompanying dependency makes these patients difficult to treat in actuality.

PSYCHOPHYSIOLOGICAL DISORDERS

In view of the actual structural changes, these disorders usually must be treated initially as a medical problem. Some patients can be helped to see the relationship between exacerbation of their symptoms and emotional upsets in their daily lives. An exploration of their present life situation is often helpful, particularly in relation to the handling of hostile feelings. Manipulation of the environment may sometimes alleviate the pressure the patient is experiencing. Resolution of the underlying personality difficulty, however, generally requires extensive psychotherapy.

HYPOCHONDRIASIS

Except for hypochondriacal concerns which arise late in life, it is extremely difficult to treat hypochondriasis. There is probably no more hostile interpersonal relationship than that between a hypochondriacal patient and a nonenlightened, nonunderstanding physician. It is an interpersonal relationship in which a mutual insecurity exists: the patient is concerned about his pain and complaints; the physician resents the presence of complaints for which he cannot find a basis and stresses that "everything is all right; you're well." Such reassurance does not help the hypochondriacal patient; if he gets a few days' magical security out of it, he will return and complain even more. It is interesting to see, at some major clinics, the hypochondriacal patients gather in the waiting room and talk over many of their complaints. This is probably as therapeutic as anything that the physician could do.

OTHER BODY-IMAGE DISTURBANCES

The range of possible disorders varies from those that can be handled by sympathetic reassurance and support by an understanding physician to those that require extensive psychiatric treatment. The physician who is aware of the sensitivities and vulnerabilities of his patient will often be able to forestall the development of more serious difficulties. For example, in addition to the normal-occurring phantom appearing with limb amputation, the painful phantom appears to arise most often when the person has not been properly prepared for the loss of the limb and the expected reactions to it. Patients about to undergo amputations are often greatly concerned about the fate of the amputated extremity. A mourning or grief reaction for the body part frequently accompanies its loss. The sensation of burning pain as the presenting symptom has been revealed in some patients to be a reflection of the fantasies about the absent extremity: "I've heard what doctors do with the organs that they take out. I know they are put in the incinerator and burned." Preparing the patient for the loss and helping him understand that the loved part of the body will be handled with respect can help to prevent such a painful reaction.

The intensity with which the patient may focus on his bodily symptoms may make it exceedingly difficult to deflect his thinking to their psychological concomitants. Some patients find security in being assured that they are physically well and that there is no organic basis for their difficulty. Such assurance can have meaning only when the physician has conveyed to the patient the total impression of competence. Reassurance based on an inadequate examination of the patient's physical and mental status can obviously mean nothing. Nevertheless, some patients must continue to hold to the belief that their difficulties are purely physical and may be extremely threatened by evidence to the contrary.

The severity of the disorders which may be expressed in body-image symptoms necessitates a careful evaluation of the patient's total functioning in the areas of both personality and physiology. In some instances, a symptom may be an expression of a transient emotional difficulty in a relatively intact personality; in other instances, the symptom may be a prodromal indication of a serious personality disintegration which may present difficult problems of management.

6

Obsessive
Reactions

One of the common personality patterns in our culture is the obsessional type, characterized by uninteresting and unimaginative attitudes, serious demeanor, devotion to hard work, and reliance on intellectual pursuits. Individuals of this type place achievement above the pursuit of pleasure and have a great desire to be respected and admired. They may appear strong-willed and overly concerned lest advantage be taken of them. They have great difficulty in being emotionally spontaneous and tend rather to be overcontrolled, inflexible, and rigid in behavior. Being orderly and perfectionistic, they may spend so much time on trifles and minutiae that attention to important matters is impossible. They are usually extremely ambivalent and may have periods of doubting and indecisiveness. Generally scrupulous in thought and behavior, they often adhere to a strict moral code, although inconsistencies may exist. They may collect objects and possessions in such a way that collection becomes an end in itself rather than a means to any intrinsic pleasure which the objects offer. Sexual pursuits tend to be pedantic and mechanical; and sex, like other activities, often becomes a highly routine (scheduled) act.

CLASSIFICATION

NORMAL VS. PATHOLOGICAL

There are obsessional components in normal personalities as well as in disturbed ones. Perseverance, reliability, and conscientiousness lend stability to the personality. Self-discipline developed as an identification with orderly and disciplined parents tends to perpetuate the healthy control and channeling of early childhood impulses. Nevertheless, it is easy to recognize that there is a fine line between healthy and neurotic traits in this aspect of personality development.

Pathological extensions of the obsessive personality may give rise to severe psychological disorders. Graduations of discipline and control range from the normal character to an adjustment characterized by a total preoccupation with repetitive thoughts and actions classed as *obsessions* and *compulsions*.

Obsession: *a recurring thought or idea which enters into consciousness without voluntary control.*

Compulsion: *a recurrent action or ritual which is repeated in a perseverative way as a means of avoiding extreme anxiety.*

Obsessions (ideas) and compulsions (actions) usually coexist so that the distinction is not invariably made and both are generally subsumed in the obsessive syndrome.

Obsessive behavior, in mild form, may be expressed in such common doubts as making "doubly sure" that the doors are locked and that the gas jets have been turned off, even after they have already been checked. In more serious forms, obsessions and compulsions can seriously affect the person's relationships to everyone about him and may leave the person unable to handle the practical problems of everyday living.

The degree of personality distortion may be a guide for classification of obsessive reactions:

OBSESSIVE PERSONALITY

The obsessive personality is typically considered within the normal range of personality, expressing obsessive patterns which may rise to worthwhile activity and achievement. Such individuals usually come to a physician when they feel they are not working at top performance or when they come to a point in early adulthood when they are not finding pleasure in life. Typical of obsessive reactions, the individual's life is often characterized by limited pleasure and enjoyment. Mild depressions may result, and the depressive component, although secondary to the obsessive reaction, may be the more prominent aspect of the patient's complaints.

OBSESSIVE-COMPULSIVE NEUROSIS

Extension of the obsessive component may give rise to specific obsessions or compulsions which interfere with the individual's carrying on normal activities. Such obsessions and compulsions reflect repetitive, intrusive impulses over which the individual has no control, although he realizes their irrational nature. Handwashing, touching, or counting rituals are common. In the obsessive-compulsive neurosis, reality testing is within normal limits.

PSYCHOSIS AND OBSESSIVE SYMPTOMS

In these instances, the basic disorder is psychotic, even though the presenting symptoms may be obsessive in nature. Obsessions and compulsions may help stabilize a basically psychotic individual, thus playing an important *defensive* role. In these instances, it is important to recognize the underlying defect in reality testing. One variety of such disorders falls in the category of "pseudoneurotic schizophrenia," a designation which reflects the fact that the presenting symptomatology is deceptive in that neurotic-like symptoms mask a psychotic (schizophrenic) disorder.

PSYCHOGENESIS

Just how do obsessional reactions develop? Most authorities would agree that the stage in personality development from which these reactions originate appears to center around bowel and habit training, the first social demands on the child. The issue at stake involves the child's own autonomy versus his giving in to others, expressed particularly around such issues as cleanliness and control of unacceptable (dirty) impulses.

In our culture, one of the first social demands of the child is cleanliness. The struggle aroused by this demand may establish reactions which persist throughout life. By the time of toilet training, the infant has already developed some patterns of eating, defecation, sexual exploration, and general behavior. Parallel to these developing functions, however, concomitantly comes the necessity for discipline, regulation, and control, particularly in a culture which places great emphasis on such values.

In response to parental demands for cleanliness and discipline, the reaction of the child may take two forms: *submission* to the demands of the parent (authority), or *defiance:*

Submission is said to result when guilt and fear predominate, giving rise to such character traits as submissiveness, conformity, orderliness, cleanliness, reliability, and conscientiousness.

Defiance is said to be the result when excessive rage predominates, giving rise to such traits as obstinacy, untidyness, negligence, and unreliability. The final resolution of this conflict is generally neither *total* submission nor *total* defiance; ultimate patterns of behavior will often reflect subtle manifestations of both reactions so that marked inconsistencies in behavior will appear later.

The struggle which ensues between the child and the parents may be an active and open struggle, or it may reveal subtle evidences of conflict. Some sensitive children never participate in an actual power struggle with the parents. Hostile feelings may be concealed in thoughts which are not expressed in action, leading to an "emotional isolation" in which feelings are habitually isolated from behavior. In other children, the conflict may lead to an open fight and direct aggression, culminating in their becoming "stubborn" and "strong-willed."

Though the child desires to be loved, he also wishes to be respected. Feeling the parents' pressure to yield to their wishes, he may become preoccupied with the task of outwitting the parents, a goal which may distort the desire to be loved into a desire to be respected and to be served. Although at first the child hopes to win this power struggle, fears of retaliation become inevitable and the *control* of rage becomes paramount, since, after all, in spite of his power he is in reality much smaller and weaker than his parents. Such a relationship with the parents may become the prototype for all other later contacts and relationships: defiance and rebellion become submerged under the pressure for submission and control.

In childhood, there may be direct derivatives of this power struggle: temper tantrums, nail-biting, bed-wetting, tics, stammering, repetitive night terrors, and rebellion against school may be manifestations of this conflict. In adulthood, the extensions of this conflict may be seen in the inhibition of the expression of direct aggression, periodic loss of self-confidence, perfectionism, overvaluation of possessions, excessive intellectual control of behavior, poor capacity for tender feelings, and the separation of feelings from thoughts.

PSYCHODYNAMICS

The defenses which the individual develops as a way of controlling his rage and the anxiety it precipitates form the basis for the extensions into adulthood of the struggle for control and can give rise to a resolution expressed and reflected in an obsessive reaction. Thus, obsessive patterns of behavior are relatively enduring ones, generally perpetuated directly from childhood into adulthood. In some instances, however, the blatant symptomatology may not occur until at some point in life when one's ongoing interpersonal relationships in some way recapitulate the original child-parent struggle centered around autonomy versus giving in to others and the control of the hostile impulses concomitant with the anxiety they arouse.

In the resultant of that behavior labeled "obsessive" or "compulsive," the mechanisms of *undoing, reaction formation,* and *isolation* usually predominate.

Undoing: *a process in which something already done (in thought or action) is symbolically canceled out (undone) as if it had never occurred.*

Many of the rituals of the obsessive individual can be understood as magical attempts to "undo" the harm the person unconsciously imagines will be caused by his wishes. "Undoing" also serves as an "excusing" function, so that punishment for hostile feelings or actions will not occur. Undoing can be seen in normal behavior in many of the religious rituals of atonement, as well as in many other conventional acts of behavior.

An example of the magic of the words "I'm sorry" was demonstrated on the beach where an older boy suddenly threw sand in the face of a small boy. For a brief moment it appeared as if the wrath of the gods were about to descend upon the boy in the form of retaliation by the parents of both children. Sensing his fate, the older boy immediately cried, "I'm sorry, I'm sorry." Peace suddenly reigned, and everyone acted as if nothing had happened.

Because the basis of obsessive rituals is established at a period of early childhood when "magical" ideas dominate, the specific meaning of the undoing mechanism in a particular adult ritual is often distorted and disguised so that it is difficult to discover its meaning.

A patient had a compulsion to count repetitively from one to five, particularly in the course of eating. The meaning of this act was revealed to be that of reassuring himself that no harm had come to any of the five members of his family toward whom he harbored unconscious murderous impulses.

Originally established as a means of controlling rage and hostile impulses aroused by parental demands, such rituals in later life serve the adaptive purpose of helping the person handle a problem in the control of hostile impulses precipitated by his present interpersonal relationships as well as the accompanying anxiety.

Another defense mechanism prominent in obsessive behavior is *reaction formation*.

Reaction formation: *an unconscious process in which behavior and attitudes are adopted that are the direct opposite of impulses which the individual cannot directly express.*

In reaction formation, one of a pair of ambivalent attitudes is reacted against by accentuation of the other. Thus, manifestations of love may be a reaction against feelings of hate; neatness and cleanliness may be a reaction against finding pleasure in dirt and messiness. Behavior which arises on the basis of a reaction-formation can usually be recognized by the exaggerated or excessive form it will take. Thus, love, which is a reaction formation against feelings of hate, may be reflected in oversolicitous care and manifestations of concern which appear inappropriate even to a casual observer. The underlying hostility is sometimes expressed by the fear that somehow the other person will be harmed; consequently, he must be cared for and protected with extreme devotion.

> A mother was so fearful that her child might be injured while crossing the street that she insisted on taking him to and from school to the age of thirteen, in spite of the fact that he was being ridiculed by other children. Her overconcern and devotion appeared to be a defense against impulses revealed in the hospital chart which stated that at the time of the child's birth, the mother had expressed the wish that her baby would die and that she had previously begged the doctors to perform an abortion.

Another clue that reaction formation is operating is that regardless of how effectively it may serve to keep the unacceptable impulse under control, the impulse will invariably reach direct expression in behavior. Thus, an isolated expression of cruelty and aggression will suddenly appear side by side with excessive love and devotion. Likewise, clean and orderly individuals may be found to retain some extremely messy habit, quite out of keeping with their total pattern of behavior. An individual who is highly fastidious about his dress and cleanliness, for example, may yet persist in carrying a very dirty handkerchief.

> An exceedingly compulsive patient placed great emphasis on cleanliness and neatness, taking at least three baths each day. Although repulsed by the idea of lying on clean sheets without first having bathed, he reported his great pleasure in the smell of foul odors, with an associated messy ritual related to bowel movements.

It is by such evidence of the fact that the original defiance was not totally submerged by submission-fear reactions that reaction formation usually can be recognized.

In addition to undoing and reaction formation, another characteristic defense of obsessional patients is *isolation*.

Isolation (*isolation of affect*): *a process by which experiences, impressions, and memories are separated from their emotional significance and are experienced without feeling or affect.*

The use of isolation deprives associations of their affective significance to such an extent that ideational content may be colorless and without emotional meaning. The rigidity, lack of spontaneity, and apparent indifference of obsessional patients reflects the degree to which isolation has become an overriding aspect of their adjustment. Isolation is apparent in obsessive rituals in which the action, conducted perfunctorily, has long since been separated from its emotional connotation. The feeling is no longer available to conscious awareness, and only the act remains. Reliance on isolation is also revealed in the emphasis which obsessional individuals place on the accumulation of factual knowledge, giving continual precedence to intellect and reason over feelings and emotions. In contrast to repression (a defense which discourages intellectuality), obsessional defenses may lead to productive, scholarly, intellectual pursuits. Less adaptively, however, they create concern with minutiae to such an extent that the individual is never really free to engage in the most important aspects of his work.

SUMMARY

The following assumptions are helpful in understanding obsessive reactions:

1. Obsessive symptomatology may occur in a variety of disorders, ranging from the normal to the psychotic.

2. Although obsessions and compulsions are typically considered as symptoms of a neurosis, they may also appear in a psychosis in which reality testing is extremely poor.

3. Obsessions and compulsions arise in terms of such defenses as: *undoing, reaction formation, isolation of affect,* and excessive reliance on *intellectualization.*

4. These defenses are utilized to control strong hostile impulses (and the accompanying anxiety) elicited around problems related to autonomy, control, and being controlled.

5. It is assumed that the obsessive syndrome was originally established in relation to the struggle with parents over bowel and habit training.

6. Recapitulation of the original conflict (control versus being controlled) in present interpersonal relationships may give rise to an exacerbation of obsessive symptomatology in adulthood.

MANAGEMENT

Obsessive defenses are generally intractable and may present a difficult problem in treatment. Since obsessional defenses have great social utility, there is much reinforcement by the environment which serves to perpetuate them. Intellectuality, for example, is admired in our culture and may be used to gain recognition and respect. Nevertheless, in the process of psychotherapy, intellectuality may be a barrier to introspection, since the individual may compulsively report factual knowledge without significant feeling. He may accept interpretations intellectually without really feeling, understanding, or accepting them in the emotional sense.

Early intervention with psychotherapy, preferably psychoanalysis, is the treatment generally considered most advisable. As extensions of the disorder occur, however, and the state of chronic and severe tension results, the positive influence of psychotherapy is less certain. The goal of treating an obsessive individual is often to help him live more comfortably with his obsessions or to help him channel his obsessiveness into productive areas. When an adjustment is precarious, obsessive defenses often serve as defenses against further regression, that is, psychosis. In such disorders, it is necessary to support obsessive defenses rather than to eliminate them or uncover their unconscious significance. Consequently, the role of obsessional defenses in the adjustment of the individual must be carefully evaluated.

7

Sexual

Disorders

A problem frequently brought to the physician is a disturbance in sexual functioning which is causing guilt, fear, or anxiety. At times, it will be the patient himself who comes to the physician to express his concern about difficulties in this highly personal area of life. On other occasions, it may be a parent, spouse, or loved one who expresses concern about the patient's sexual difficulties.

Due to the fact that our culture places great value on sexual attractiveness and sexual potency, it sometimes appears that a patient's feelings of worth and self-esteem totally depend upon how adequately he functions in the sexual act. Perhaps our culture places undue emphasis on sex in this era of compulsive sexuality. It is, for example, a fairly recent innovation that increasing emphasis is placed on the desirability of satisfying the sexual partner. Indeed, it has been said that some individuals have become so imbued with the importance of this goal that for them the sexual act represents a challenge to demonstrate their competence to such an extent that the enjoyment of both partners is diminished.

Since it is possibly the most intimate of any interpersonal relationship, the sexual act often highlights problems which actually characterize all of the person's relationships. Therefore, although the patient's complaint may appear to be solely related to sexual matters, it is more usual to find that it represents merely one aspect of what is a more generalized maladaptive pattern of adjustment.

CLASSIFICATION

Sexual disorders and aberrations in sexual functioning may take many forms. Some of the sexual problems frequent in our culture include:

Homosexuality: sexual attraction to a member of one's own sex, usually implying a desire for or actual participation in overt sexual contact. Homosexual impulses may also be unconscious and may give rise to sublimated activities or to conflict in which the sexual significance is not immediately apparent.

Voyeurism: a disorder in which abnormal gratification is achieved by "peeping." This activity, as a perversion, is carried on in a clandestine fashion and is usually accompanied by masturbation.

Exhibitionism: a disorder in which abnormal gratification is achieved through intentional exposure of the sex organs in inappropriate circumstances. This disorder is most commonly found in males who expose themselves to women, adolescent girls, or very young children.

Fetishism: a disorder in which sexual excitement and gratification are produced by an object which is invested with abnormal sexual significance and love (e.g., a lock of hair, a stocking, a brassiere).

Transvestism: the act of dressing in clothes of the opposite sex, usually found in men and often carried out in a ritual involving masturbation.

Potency Difficulties: difficulties in achieving successful culmination of the sexual act. Common complaints include impotence (inability to achieve and maintain an erection), premature or retarded ejaculation in the male; frigidity (inability to achieve orgasm) and vaginismus (involuntary painful spasm of the vaginal muscles) in the female.

Upon initial presentation by the patient, the symptom's significance in the total organization of the patient's personality is often difficult to infer. Sexual problems, like other symptoms, serve many functions. In many patients, a sexual disorder may be a relatively circumscribed problem in an otherwise intact and effectively functioning individual. In other patients, the symptom may indicate a disorganization of personality which upon close inspection is seen to be psychotic. Likewise, a given problem in one patient may be transient and easily modified by external circumstances; in another patient, it may be extremely intractable. For example, many adults have been sexually impotent while experiencing a debilitating cold, or even when unduly tired or temporarily depressed. Nevertheless, as a persistent problem, potency difficulties are extremely difficult to relieve and often require extensive and intensive psychotherapy.

When evaluating the patient's complaints, the examiner must be aware of the cultural attitudes which color the patient's ideation and report, as well as of his own biases and attitudes regarding sexual matters. In problems related to sex, it is often more difficult to draw a definitive line between what is deviant or abnormal and what is within normal limits than in any other area of human behavior. Certain acts which may constitute part of the foreplay in the sexual act, for example, become pathological only when they constitute the end-goal in themselves. Cultural attitudes also are constantly shifting; consequently, what might appear grossly abnormal in one setting at one time may appear much less so in other circumstances.

The difficulties in making such distinctions can be illustrated by the problem of homosexuality. Although most people think of a dichotomy which separates the homosexual from the heterosexual, the picture is actually more complex. For example, psychoanalytic theory postulates a homosexual phase of adjustment in normal preadolescence during which the young boy or girl has almost exclusive interest in members of his or her own sex. It is also relevant to note that studies have indicated that over one-third of the males and one-fourth of the females reported the occurrence after the onset of adolescence of some form of homosexual release to the point of orgasm. Thus, many individuals who have had homosexual experiences are not homosexual in the sense of its constituting a single method of sexual expression. As one becomes aware of the motivational aspects of behavior, one also sees that some behavior (such as Don Juanism) which might appear solely heterosexual is motivated by underlying homosexual impulses. Complicating the issue even further, both homosexual and heterosexual behavior may be motivated by nonsexual impulses (e.g., competitive strivings, dependency satisfactions, hostility), the sexual component being secondary. Hence, a patient's report that he has a "homosexual problem" must, like any other complaint, be carefully investigated rather than interpreted in terms of one's own stereotypes.

PSYCHODYNAMICS

As already indicated in the discussion under "classification," sexual symptoms can serve many purposes and can be generated by quite different motivations. No one mechanism invariably gives rise to a particular form of sexual disturbance. Protracted sexual disturbances usually have exceedingly complex determinants, and there are no exclusive psychodynamics for any of the symptoms listed in the descriptive category of a "sexual disorder"; nevertheless, certain basic issues are frequent components of the underlying psychodynamics.

HOSTILITY

As part of the complex motivations that comprise the determinant of sexual difficulties, unconscious hostility may be a significant component. Sexual behavior may also be a means of expressing unconscious hostility to the partner, often with a need to derogate or frustrate the partner in the sexual act. This derogation or frustration may be in symbolic or direct form. Homosexual love in the male, for example, often has its genesis in a need to deny or react against tremendous feelings of hostility, competition, and rivalry toward a person of the same sex, frequently originally a brother or father. The homosexual act of a male may symbolically serve the unconscious need for "killing off" another male by rendering him impotent sexually. Similarly in premature ejaculation, the male may be expressing derision toward the female, denying her satisfaction and spilling the semen on her as if it were urine, or expressing hostility to her by depriving her of the pleasure of orgasm. In certain kinds of voyeurism, "peeping" is fantasied as an assertive, defiant act which is invested with strong hostile overtones. Sex is sometimes directly fused with hostility, with the sex act consciously or unconsciously conceived of as an attack. One's own hostility may give rise to fears of being hurt, as well as of hurting someone else, as punishment for harboring such unacceptable impulses.

DEPENDENCY

The sexual disturbance may be the result of forces which include strong dependency motivations. The man who as a child has learned that sex is "dirty," and thus not something his mother would enjoy, may imbue women with the qualities of his mother and thus be unable to have sexual relations with them. Some men, for example, can be potent only with prostitutes, having dichotomized womanhood into two groups (the saint-sinner dichotomy): those who are "good" women like one's mother versus those who are "bad," with whom one can consequently enjoy sex. In certain forms of homosexuality, dependency gratifications are achieved through the symbolic equation of the penis with the breast. The sex act itself (in either homosexual or heterosexual form) may be equated with taking a dependent, subservient position. The need to be dependent and cared for may take precedence over the desire for mature sexual relations as a mature partner.

UNCONSCIOUS HOMOSEXUALITY

Strong unconscious homosexual impulses may be operating without the person's awareness of them and may give rise to difficulties in heterosexual functioning, e.g., impotence and premature ejaculation. A need to deny and react against unconscious unacceptable homosexual impulses may also give rise to Don Juanism, an exaggerated heterosexual façade in which sex is engaged in compulsively with many different partners. Exaggerated heterosexual activity may thus be a reaction against underlying feelings of weakness, impotence, and passivity. In other instances, a preference for sexual partners who are known to be promiscuous may be based on the link to members of one's own sex, which the partner represents unconsciously. Sexual acting-out, in which a partner is shared with members of one's own sex, may thus have homosexual implications, although the behavior is all seemingly heterosexual. Anxiety about being a homosexual may disrupt sexual functioning or the enjoyment of it. Such anxiety may be precipitated by the individual's failure to reach some nonsexual goal which nevertheless is equated in our culture with being "feminine" or "masculine." Business failure or any competitive defeat may in the male, for example, be equated with being a failure, hence "feminine" and "homosexual." Such anxiety has sometimes been labeled "pseudo-homosexual anxiety" since it is precipitated by nonsexual goals, rather than truly homosexual motivations.

CASTRATION ANXIETY

Castration anxiety subsumes unconscious fears of bodily damage, often expressed in fears or feelings of being castrated, either symbolically or literally. Underlying fear of being hurt or damaged may lead to an acceleration of the sex act culminating in premature ejaculation. Castration anxiety may also motivate other behavior. For many male homosexuals, the sight of female genitals is extremely repulsive and anxiety-producing, as it proves that people without a penis actually do exist, reinforcing their underlying fears of what could happen to them. Hence they feel safe only with those who like themselves have a penis. The homosexual act may also be "reparative," in the sense that it symbolically serves as a means by which the individual appropriates to himself the strength (and potency) of his partner. Such "undoing" of castration may occur in other rituals: the exhibitionist utilizes genital exposure to elicit a reaction of astonishment or admiration, seeking, it appears, reassurance that his penis is still there; the voyeur, while dangerously skirting the confrontation of the absent penis in women, usually manages assiduously to avoid seeing that specific part of the female's anatomy; the person engaging in fetishism, generally with an object phallic in shape or significance, is likewise (among other things) attempting to deny and react against underlying castration anxiety. In our culture, being a male offers many prerogatives other than those that are specifically sexual. "Penis envy" in the female may give rise to feelings of envy, competition, and hostility which are expressed in the sexual act itself as well as in other areas of functioning.

MISPLACED IDENTIFICATION

Sexual difficulties may arise because the individual identifies, in fact or in fantasy, with the role that is appropriate for the opposite sex. For the male, the appropriate role typically involves playing the active, intrusive part in the sexual act; for the female, this role typically involves greater receptivity and passivity. If identification becomes displaced, the motivation may be to enjoy the sexual act in a manner similar to the experience of the person of the opposite sex. If the underlying sexual impulse or fantasy is not consistent with the roles actually demanded by normal heterosexual activities, difficulties arise which may be expressed in impotency, the need for unusual stimulation (such as enabling fantasies), lack of sexual enjoyment, and other sexual symptoms.

PSYCHOGENESIS

The psychogenesis of protracted sexual disturbances is frequently found in extremely early life experiences, usually those within the family. The basis for such disturbances may be laid by disruption in the establishment of patterns for dependency gratifications, assertive capacities, and a sense of identity of one's sex. Identification with the roles of the parents is dependent upon a model of the same sex whom one can emulate and whom one ultimately chooses to be like. In the male child, the process of normal identification is disrupted, for example, if the father figure is frequently absent, is a weak or inadequate model who does not himself enjoy the role of the male, or is perceived by the growing child as a distant, cruel, threatening figure. In such instances, the boy may identify more predominantly with the mother, ultimately coming to a final resolution in which sex is enjoyed in a way similar to the way in which he fantasies the mother enjoyed it. In like manner, the growing girl must have an appropriate female model with whom she can identify if she is ultimately going to be able to fulfill her role as a female with enjoyment and satisfaction. If parents are themselves happy and well adjusted in their role as male and female, children will normally come to appropriate roles befitting their own sex. As will be discussed later (Chapter 8), some sexual acting out in children and adolescents has its genesis in response to the parents' unconscious impulses leading to behavior which gives vicarious gratification to the parent by fulfilling the image he actually holds for the child. This may be particularly true if one or both parents actually wished for a child of the opposite sex.

Numerous cultural factors also contribute to the genesis of common sexual disturbances. Sex is frequently taboo in our culture and is depicted as "dirty," "sinful," "dangerous," generally as something not to be discussed. The growing child often labors under much misinformation and many misconceptions regarding sex, pregnancy, and childbirth. Threats are frequently extended to normal bodily functions such as masturbation, with verbalized warnings to the child that he will be damaged or that his mind will be affected if he engages in the practice. Exhibitionistic or voyeuristic impulses which are normal in certain stages of the child's growth may be perverted by the parents' response to the child's innocent and natural behavior. Since the opportunity for normal, sanctioned sexual experiences in our culture is limited, sex may take on many meanings which have little to do with the sex act itself.

Although the dangers of excessive repression are generally obvious in our culture, unlimited freedom pertaining to sexual matters does not prove to be an ideal alternative. Dangers may also exist if a child is overly stimulated at an age when he cannot give appropriate expression to his impulses. Some parents, under the guise of being "uninhibited" and "liberated" about sex, engage in behavior very damaging to the child by going about inappropriately undressed or seductively clothed, or by otherwise being sexually provocative. Retrospective histories of patients with sexual perversions reveal the extent to which parents have participated in the formation of the perversion, often by behavior which may be rationalized with explanations such as, "After all, the body is nothing of which to be ashamed," or, "Sex is a natural, normal experience." These explanations, while indeed literally true, should not obscure the degree to which such parents may be collaborating in a way so as to deprive the child of a healthy sexual adjustment in a culture which maintains certain standards and values regarding sexual behavior.

The greatest likelihood that a child will not develop serious sexual disturbances in later life probably prevails if the parents themselves have a happy, normal sexual adjustment with each other and are happy in their own roles as man and woman. Such a model probably transcends in importance all other conditions: one does not need to know, for example, all the intimate details of male and female anatomy for a normal sexual adjustment to occur—knowing all "the facts of life" may be relatively unimportant. Likewise, such experiences as an incidental homosexual seduction will not be crucial if the appropriate model has been provided by parents. If parents are themselves well adjusted, then appropriate standards will be maintained without perpetuating irrational fears and anxieties about sex, with the child coming ultimately to develop confidence and respect for his body and pleasure and competence in normal sexual experiences.

SUMMARY

The following assumptions are helpful in understanding sexual disorders:

1. Sexual problems, like other symptoms, can serve many functions.

2. Although the patient's complaint may appear to be solely related to sexual matters, it may actually represent merely one aspect of a more generalized maladaptive pattern of adjustment.

3. Although the psychodynamic determinants for protracted sexual disturbances are complex, significant influences frequently include such factors as hostility, dependency, unconscious homosexuality, "castration anxiety," and misplaced identification.

4. Although many other explanations have been offered for the genesis of the more typical sexual disturbances, including explanations pertaining to constitutional and genetic factors, the consensus of most authorities would relate such disturbances to early familial and cultural influences, particularly in relation to parental figures.

MANAGEMENT

Although protracted sexual disturbances may require extensive psychotherapy for successful alleviation of the disorder, there are many practical aspects of management which should be commented upon. Since anxiety often directly interferes with successful sexual functioning, any maneuvers that diminish the intensity of the patient's anxiety are beneficial. Drugs may be useful for this purpose; although, if the rationale for their use is not made explicit to the patient, they may support the erroneous impression that the difficulty is a physical one. Reassurance and support by an understanding, sympathetic physician may be of inestimable value. In an era of presumed sexual enlightenment, the degree of misinformation and ignorance about sexual matters is enormous. The physician's role is often necessarily that of an educator. He may also help alleviate feelings of guilt about impulses which may not be nearly so unusual or different as the patient believes. The physician himself must avoid being judgmental, recognizing that a wide latitude of opinion exists in defining what is normal. He may help place sex in proper perspective, assisting the patient to recognize that one's total self-esteem should not be based solely on one's sexual functioning. It is often relatively easy to demonstrate to a patient that his sexual inadequacies parallel inadequacies and difficulties in other spheres; e.g., vocational, financial. This may deemphasize the specific sexual aspects of the patient's problems. Long-term psychotherapy is offering increasingly better prognoses in such disturbances as homosexuality and transvestism, although the patient's basic desire to change is a prerequisite for successful treatment.

An issue which must sometimes be considered in relationship to management is whether the patient's behavior is a danger to himself or to others. Patients' ability to control their inappropriate sexual impulses varies greatly, dependent not exclusively upon their ability to evaluate reality. Such factors as their ability to tolerate tension, to postpone gratification, to experience guilt, and to recognize the consequences of their behavior are also involved. Prevailing attitudes about the expression of particular sexual impulses are also relevant. For example, while society may be relatively tolerant about homosexual activities occurring between adults if carried on discretely, it generally does not approve of sexual activities between adult and child. Although authorities agree that sexual intercourse between fathers and their daughters is probably more common than is generally supposed, there is a general feeling that children and certain other classes of individuals must be protected from being sexually exploited by adults.

8

Disorders of Conscience

Subsumed by the category of disorders of conscience are numerous disturbances in social adjustment characterized by amoral or antisocial behavior which is engaged in with a minimal conflict, guilt, or sense of responsibility. Although it includes grossly disparate groups of persons, this category is restricted to individuals whose behavioral patterns lack the traditional characteristics of a neurosis or a psychosis. These individuals persistently engage in amoral acts while knowing and understanding the implications of their behavior and in spite of the social consequences. In doing so, they experience minimal personal discomfort or regrets. Anxiety and depression, if present, relate more to their fear of being or having been caught than to any intrinsic guilt over having committed the act. These individuals are often above average in intelligence and know the difference between right and wrong. They are generally indifferent to what other people think, however, and tend to develop extremely superficial relationships. While they may be popular socially, their relationships lack stability because of their impaired capacity to form affectional ties. Their behavior is characterized by a lack of long-range goals, inability to learn from experience, and their ability to tolerate tension and frustration is extremely poor.

Behavioral patterns included in this category typically include chronic lying and cheating, truancy, forgery, stealing, overt hostility and destructiveness, fire setting, and sexual promiscuity. In some instances, such disorders as drug addiction, alcoholism, and certain sexual disturbances also fall in this general category.

CLASSIFICATION

The patterns of behavior described herein, when not occurring in the presence of a discrete neurosis or psychosis, have sometimes been classified as "psychopathic personality" or "character disorder." Because such behavior has often appeared to be exempt from the usual effects of reward and punishment, it was assumed at one time that a strong constitutional factor must underlie the disorder, an assumption reflected in an alternative designation, "constitutional psychopathic inferior." Although fewer authorities would now accept this assumption in view of recent findings suggesting the role of specific environmental influences, this older designation does reflect the difficulty that existed in the past in understanding behavior for which the potential punishment seemed to exceed the potential reward in individuals who presumably knew "better" or knew "right from wrong."

It should be made explicit that any of these delinquent acts can arise in the context of specific neurotic, psychotic, or organic determinants, a possibility which must always be carefully evaluated. For example, a person may be a mental defective and engage in stealing largely because he does not know any better. He may suffer brain damage and likewise become, in society's sense, "not responsible." Stealing may also arise in the presence of defective reality-testing indicative of a psychosis, or it may serve unconscious symbolic purposes as one symptom among many in an ongoing neurosis. In the latter instance in particular, there are generally accompanying guilt, anxiety, remorse, depression, and doubt. The occurrence of delinquent behavior in a person in whom mental deficiency, brain damage, psychosis, and neurosis have all been ruled out is much more difficult to explain or comprehend. As a diagnosis traditionally made by the process of exclusion, the so-called "psychopathic personality" at one time consequently appeared to reflect behavior which was without sufficient motivation and which represented somewhat of an etiological mystery.

PSYCHOGENESIS

There is no common agreement on the major etiological factor in delinquent, antisocial, or criminal behavior. Undoubtedly the lack of agreement stems largely from the fact that the determinants are extremely varied and complex and that delinquent behavior, as any other symptom, is multidetermined.

Some authorities assume a strong *constitutional* factor in the etiology of these behavioral disorders. Evidence for this viewpoint is constituted by findings which reveal a high correlation of body build (mesomorphic type) with antisocial behavior. Some investigators also have found a much higher incidence of abnormal electroencephalograms than occur in the normal population. Nevertheless, in spite of such sporadic findings, no evidence of somatic pathology has been found on routine physical or laboratory investigations in the majority of individuals who manifest defects in conscience. For those authorities who nevertheless maintain the belief that there is an hereditary or constitutional inferiority, the intractable nature of these disorders is taken as supporting evidence for their view.

For those authorities who stress the *experiential* contribution to the etiology of the disorder, numerous studies point up a greater statistical frequency of broken homes, missing parents, illegitimate births, and emotional and socioeconomic deprivation in the backgrounds of those who engage in antisocial behavior. For example, a repeated finding is that mother-child separation for an extended period before the age of six years is a much more frequent occurrence in those children who later become antisocial. Some authorities are willing to assume that maternal deprivation is a major factor in antisocial behavior, in spite of the fact that it does not invariably result in this outcome.

It is generally recognized that the development of a conscience (superego) does not occur automatically; neither is it present at birth. In the process of socialization, the child comes to accept and develop the value systems which are represented to him by significant individuals around him. Some authorities believe that a crucial stage in the development of the conscience is around four to five years of age, when the child is experiencing impulses which are assumed to be broadly sexual in nature. It is at this time, it is believed, that direct fulfillment must de denied, with the solution coming through an acceptance of parental attitudes as one's own. In any event, regardless of the exact motivating forces, the child ultimately achieves desirable patterns of behavior through imitating, emulating, and identifying with the models presented to him.

The factors which may disturb this process of socialization are numerous. If the child feels rejected, he may desire to disgrace or punish his rejecting parents or to seek self-punishment as expiation for the guilt of having angry feelings toward them. Deprivation may also lead to patterns of behavior which emphasize immediate gratification and getting whatever one can whenever there is the opportunity. It is possible, on the other hand, that overindulgence may also perpetuate patterns of egocentricity and disregard for the rights of others, since the child does not have the opportunity to learn to delay gratification or to tolerate the tensions that arise when one's personal needs are not immediately satisfied.

Certain kinds of delinquency can be explained fairly easily in the light of the unsatisfactory identification models that are provided. If parents themselves obviously lie, cheat, steal, or deceive, it is easy to recognize that the child consequently may come to behave in a similar fashion without any feeling of remorse or guilt. Likewise, certain forms of social or "gang" delinquency, occurring particularly in the lower socioeconomic groups, can be understood as identification with models that are clearly represented to the child in that particular culture.

Not all forms of antisocial behavior, however, are so easily understood. In many instances, the establishment of delinquency patterns is a much less obvious process, occurring in settings which do not obviously foster such a development.

The subtlety of the process by which antisocial behavior may be initiated and fostered has become increasingly clarified, owing largely to the collaborative studies of parents and their children, who engaged in specific antisocial behavior.[1] These studies have shown the ways in which *antisocial acting out in children is often unconsciously initiated, fostered, and encouraged by parents who vicariously achieve gratification of their own poorly integrated impulses through the child's behavior.* The interchanges between the parent and child may serve the further purpose of allowing one or both parents to express the hostility inherent in their own conflicts in a fashion destructive to the child. This is sometimes so thoroughly accomplished by the parents that they literally allow the child to destroy himself.

In order to learn the psychodynamic forces behind this process, it is helpful to understand the development of a normal conscience and normal guilt feelings, including the subtle conscious and unconscious ways by which the parents' standards direct the development of the child's behavior.

Identification consists of more than copying the verbalized standards of the parent by the child. It is also something more than simply emulating the parents' overt behavior. Identification also involves inclusion of the subtleties of the parents' conscious and unconscious image of the child. A healthy mother assumes that her child will be

---

[1] Although many individuals have contributed to these endeavors, Doctors S. A. Szurek and Adelaide Johnson must be especially mentioned (see Bibliography). The specific hypothesis discussed above appears to have been first stated explicitly by Szurek and later elaborated upon by Johnson and her co-workers. The resulting formulation of the psychogenesis of antisocial acting out in children and adolescents is sometimes referred to as the "Johnson-Szurek hypothesis." The above description of how the process occurs borrows heavily from the writings of these investigators.

law-abiding and moral. If an order is given or a prohibition made, it is taken for granted that the child will obey. Prohibitions are made only when relevant and do not suggest to the child previously unrecognized possibilities about how he might misbehave.

In parents of children who engage in amoral or antisocial behavior, a different process is sometimes discernible upon prolonged investigation. The mother, who assumes that her child may be something other than moral and law-abiding, repeatedly conveys this unstated alternative to the child. While the child may identify with the verbalized prohibition, he also identifies with the alternative image in the parents' thoughts. Sensing the peculiar emotional need conveyed in the tone of the parents' expression, he identifies not only with the positively consistent attitudes of the parent but also with the frequently unexpressed ambivalent, antisocial fantasy and expectation.

Parental prohibitions may themselves serve to inform the child of previously unknown ways of behaving.

> A twenty-year-old male homosexual patient, engaging also infrequently in voyeuristic activities, reported he first became consciously attracted to the possibilities of homosexual behavior at the age of eleven or twelve when he had been visiting another boy and had stayed past his usual bedtime. The patient's parents presumably appeared at the windows of the friend's home and, after attempting to see what was going on inside, angrily called their boy outside and verbalized their suspicions about the sexual play they presumed had been occurring. The patient reported that at this time he was not only innocent of the accusations but that he did not even fully understand them, as the thought of sexual activity with his friend had not previously entered his mind. The mother was constantly preoccupied with the fear that her children might be "sex deviants." Nevertheless, the children were excluded from the frequent showing of pornographic movies brought for evening entertainment by an uncle.

> Another homosexual patient reported that as long as he could remember, a repeated warning of his mother was that she would die if he were ever to become a homosexual.

In spite of the high-sounding morality which such parents may verbalize, close inspection frequently reveals glaring defects in their own moral code. Such defects have been referred to as "superego lacunae," a designation which suggests that although the conscience or superego is basically sound, numerous gaps in moral standards also prevail. These lacunae may serve as a clue to the unconscious impulses which are actually directing the expression of the child's behavior.

> A father, after punishing his boy in a most severe form for having stolen some nails, proceeded to use the nails to repair the porch steps rather than insisting that the nails be returned to their rightful owner.

> Although taking extremely punitive action against a child for having spent a few pennies which were not rightfully his, a father described his own clever ability to cheat the government on income tax. He was inordinately proud of his large collection of hotel towels, accumulated in his travels around the country.

The sanction may be conveyed to the child in subtle but nonverbal communication often, for example, in approving looks or expressions. Collaborative studies have emphasized the importance of nonverbal communication in directing the child's behavior. An entranced expression on the face of the parent as a child is reporting a hostile act to his teacher may be sufficient to inform the child that the parent is achieving some enjoyable gratification, regardless of what the parent may later indicate through verbal or physical threats.

> The relevance of the Johnson-Szurek hypothesis first became apparent in the case of a seventeen-year-old transvestite when the investigator was subjectively struck by the feeling that the mother enjoyed telling the story of her son's misbehavior. Without request, the mother also presented a long, detailed, and typewritten account of the boy's activities in carbon form, as the original copy was being shared elsewhere. The boy's ritual included wearing his mother's clothes, invariably left so that his mother would recognize that this had occurred. The mother had separated from her husband at the time of the boy's birth, ostensibly because she had found the clothing of another woman in her bed when she returned from the hospital following delivery. She later indicated that she really did not mind her husband's "running around" but she "couldn't take his beatings." It appeared significant that in his sexual ritual, the boy was persist-

ently acting in a way so that he, like the father, would be detected by the mother.

As a result of collaborative studies of such children and their parents, there is felt to be much less of a mystery about the etiology of these disorders than existed in the past.

Psychodynamics

The psychodynamics of disorders of conscience have already been implied in the discussion under psychogenesis. When antisocial behavior occurs outside the context of specific neurotic, psychotic, or organic determinants, investigation usually discloses that effective superego functioning has simply never developed. Because this failure in learning is perpetuated from childhood directly into adulthood, the adult behavior may be without apparent motivation in terms of the immediate present. Hence, with such disorders it is sometimes more difficult to isolate psychodynamics from psychogenesis. Nevertheless, it can be recognized that behavior, originally established in terms of the parents' unconscious, forbidden impulses, can be perpetuated throughout life, even when the original parents are no longer present. Parental surrogates and alternative authority figures may play a similar reinforcing role to behavior which, although explicitly condemned, is at the same time implicitly condoned. Inconsistencies in our cultural mores and even in religious standards may help perpetuate such behavior, as ready rationalizations are always available. Unlike the neurosis or psychosis which brings discomfort and suffering to the patient, the behavior described herein often brings immediate satisfactions which continue to serve as reinforcing agents to patterns of behavior established early in life.

In some instances, however, individuals who are extremely clever at committing some antisocial act will nevertheless, through inadvertent and often foolish error, succeed in getting caught or being detected. They may leave evidence behind in the otherwise "perfect" crime. The carelessness revealed in the errors supports the impression that there may be vestiges of an extremely repressed or unconscious guilt which leads the patient to get caught so that he may be punished.

SUMMARY

The following assumptions are helpful in understanding disorders of conscience:

1. Antisocial, delinquent, or "psychopathic" behavior may arise in the context of discernible neurotic, psychotic, or organic determinants. On the other hand, it may appear to be "unmotivated," in the sense that sufficient determinants are not readily discernible.

2. The primary defect in individuals who persistently engage in behavior of this type is related to the formation of a conscience (or superego). Since a conscience is developed largely through a child's interaction with parental figures, many authorities consider the child-parent relationship the major determinant in the genesis of antisocial behavior.

3. Recent investigations have clarified the extremely subtle influences which determine the child's acting out, indicating how some antisocial behavior may unwittingly be initiated, fostered, and reinforced by basically law-abiding parents whose own unacceptable impulses are being expressed by the child.

4. Antisocial behavior has extremely complex multideterminants.

MANAGEMENT

Therapy in such disorders is very difficult; long-term patterns of antisocial behavior are often most resistive to change. Chance of successful treatment is obviously better in those instances when it is begun early, especially if attempts are to be made to disengage the child's behavior from the parents' reinforcing maneuvers. Needless to say, however, a parent who receives desired gratification, albeit unconsciously, is not eager to remove the source of his satisfaction.

Likewise, a child who is attempting to satisfy parental wishes is not motivated to seek a change that will drive the needed parent away from him.

Authorities who have worked most extensively with these disorders in children recommend a collaborative therapy in which both child and parent are treated individually with close interchange between the therapists. Material pertinent to the current problem is discussed openly between the therapists and the patients, if it is useful to do so. Emphasis is placed on setting specific limits upon the antisocial behavior. Such limits must be drawn at the appropriate times and in view of the mutual understanding of the parent-child interactions.

A special problem is that the therapist himself may acquire vicarious gratification, particularly when the patient's exploits are in the sexual sphere. Some therapists, by failing to draw prohibitions to behavior, may unwittingly foster the acting out, just as the parent originally did. It must thus be recognized that proper and meaningful prohibitions may generate a feeling of security in the patient who unknowingly is being driven to behavior which may contain elements of his own destruction.

For successful treatment to occur in the antisocial adult, he must have a strong desire to change his patterns of behavior. This may occur only after society has enforced punishment upon him, often after it is too late. Such patients usually do not seek treatment, however, nor do they desire to change. Unlike the typical neurotic or psychotic individual, their own internal suffering is minimal. As stated previously, their anxiety or depression invariably relates more to their fear of being or having been caught than to any personal sense of responsibility, guilt, or conscience. While some success has been reported with the plan of consistent therapeutic discipline in a controlled environment, supplemented by individual or group psychotherapy, many therapists are pessimistic about the attempts to change the truly antisocial individual when such behavior occurs outside the usual confines of specific neurotic, psychotic, or organic determinants.

9

Disorders of Intelligence
(Mental Retardation)

Mental retardation refers to those abnormal conditions characterized by a defect in intellectual development which generally exists at birth or arises in early childhood and is induced by disease, injury, genetic disturbances, or extreme social deprivation. It includes those conditions variously classified as *mental deficiency, feeblemindedness, mental subnormality,* and *amentia.*

The primary disturbance of mental retardation is arrested or retarded intellectual development. Although the clinical manifestations may present signs and symptoms not directly related to functions and abilities subsumed by the concept of "intelligence," these manifestations are secondary to the primary intellectual deficit. In some instances, external physical anomalies accompany the disorder.

CLASSIFICATION

The psychological classification of mental deficiency is determined by the degree of intellectual impairment or deficit that exists: severe, moderate, or mild. In terms of the standard measure of intellectual ability (IQ),[1] *severe* refers to individuals with IQ's below 50; *moderate* refers to IQ's of 50 to 69; and *mild* refers to IQ's of 70 to 85. Some authorities would prefer classifying this latter group (70 to 85) as "borderline" rather than specifically labeling it as a degree of mental retardation. The terms "moron," "imbecile," and "idiot," to designate IQ categories of 50 to 69, 20 to 49, and below 20, respectively, are generally no longer in usage.

Estimation of the degree of impairment should include other parameters than the Intelligence Quotient. The adaptability of the individual to his particular cultural and social environment also must be evaluated. The social, educational, and vocational effectiveness of individuals with the same IQ may be different, with implications for management and prognosis which vary greatly. Although scales exist for evaluating the individual's adaptive behavior (e.g., the Vineland Social Maturity Scale), judgment of the individual's ability to meet the standards of personal independent and social

---

[1] The IQ (Intelligence Quotient) is a statistical concept expressed in a score on an intelligence test which compares the individual's performance on selected intellectual tasks with the performance achieved by a standardization group chosen as presumably being representative of the general population. Early formalized attempts at measuring intelligence established the IQ as a measure which related the child's mental age (the child's level of development expressed as equivalent to the life-age at which the average child attains that level) and the child's true chronological age. Thus, IQ equals mental age divided by chronological age. As applied to the measurement of adult intelligence, however, this ratio is misleading, since the average adult does not show an increase in test performance proportional to his increasing chronological age much beyond the age of 14. Consequently, present intelligence tests for adults directly compare the individual's performance with that of a group his own age. As a statistical derivation in terms of IQ, the classification "mental defective" on the most widely used individual intelligence test is limited to 2.2 per cent of the population. For those interested in the theoretical or practical aspects of measuring intelligence, see the Bibliography.

responsibility expected for his age remains subjective and must be made relative to the particular environment in which the individual is expected to function.

Although the IQ is important in the determination of mental retardation, it must be made explicit that many individuals may be functioning at a comparably low intellectual level because of conditions other than mental retardation per se. These conditions may be temporary (e.g., drug reaction, exhaustion, acute brain syndromes) or permanent (e.g., irreparable emotional trauma, chronic brain syndromes associated with brain trauma, senile brain disease, intracranial neoplasm). In true mental retardation, however, the following two conditions generally prevail:

1. There is no evidence that the individual functioned at a normal level of intelligence beyond the time when normal developmental skills are acquired. (This factor makes it easy to rule out mental retardation in disorders beginning later in life, although it often does not help differentiate mental retardation from childhood schizophrenia, a differentiation which is often difficult to make in the young child who may be functioning intellectually at the mental defective level.) [2]

2. The defect is a fairly global one in that it affects all areas of intellectual functioning. Variability in functioning (e.g., functioning normally in some areas but defectively in others), on the other hand, is much more characteristic of impairment due to a functional disorder or to a brain syndrome acquired some time after normal verbal and motor skills were already acquired. For this reason, the IQ as the sole index of intellectual functioning has distinct limitations, unless the total pattern of intellectual functioning in terms of relative strengths and weaknesses is spelled out.

---

[2] Ultimate elimination of these disorders will be greatly facilitated by careful etiological delineation of these groups. Nevertheless, in terms of available state institutions for such children, the alternative is often state mental hospitals or state schools for the mentally retarded. As facilities for training and management are often superior in the state schools, practical recommendations are frequently made solely in terms of the child's level of intellectual performance, regardless of the above distinctions.

ETIOLOGY [3]

Although not all forms of mental deficiency are of known etiology, a large percentage can be traced directly to known causes, either endogenous (inherent in the genetic constitution) or exogenous (environmental).

The simplified medical classification offered by the American Association on Mental Deficiency [4] provides an outline of the wide range of disorders which can give rise to mental retardation.

Simplified Medical Classification

I

Mental retardation associated with diseases and conditions due to infection:

> Encephalopathy, congenital, associated with prenatal infection
> Encephalopathy due to postnatal cerebral infection

II

Mental retardation associated with diseases and conditions due to intoxication:

> Encephalopathy, congenital, associated with toxemia of pregnancy
> Encephalopathy, congenital, associated with other maternal intoxications
> Bilirubin encephalopathy (Kernicterus)
> Post-immunization encephalopathy
> Encephalopathy, other, due to intoxication

III

Mental retardation associated with diseases and conditions due to trauma or physical agent:

> Encephalopathy due to prenatal injury
> Encephalopathy due to mechanical injury at birth
> Encephalopathy due to asphyxia at birth
> Encephalopathy due to postnatal injury

---

[3] Since psychological disorders play minor (if not nonexistent) roles in the etiology of true mental deficiency, the terms "psychogenesis" and "psychodynamics" are not appropriate in a discussion of the primary causes of the disorder.

[4] "A Manual on Terminology and Classification in Mental Retardation," Monograph Supplement No. 1, *American Journal of Mental Deficiency*, September, 1959, pp. 10–12.

IV

Mental retardation associated with diseases and conditions due to disorder of metabolism, growth, or nutrition:

Cerebral lipoidosis, infantile (Tay-Sach's disease)
Encephalopathy associated with other disorders of lipoid metabolism
Phenylketonuria
Encephalopathy associated with other disorders of protein metabolism
Galactosemia
Encephalopathy associated with other disorders of carbohydrate metabolism
Arachnodactyly
Hypothyroidism
Gargoylism (Lipochondrodystrophy)
Encephalopathy, other, due to metabolic, growth, or nutritional disorder

V

Mental retardation associated with diseases and conditions due to new growths:

Neurofibromatosis (von Recklinghausen's disease)
Trigeminal cerebral angiomatosis (Sturge-Weber-Dimitri's disease)
Tuberous sclerosis
Intracranial neoplasm, other

VI

Mental retardation associated with diseases and conditions due to (unknown) prenatal influence:

Cerebral defect, congenital
Encephalopathy associated with primary cranial anomaly
Laurence-Moon-Biedl syndrome
Mongolism
Other, due to unknown prenatal influence

VII

Mental retardation associated with diseases and conditions due to unknown or uncertain cause with the structural reactions manifest:

Encephalopathy associated with diffuse sclerosis of brain
Encephalopathy associated with cerebellar degeneration
Encephalopathy, other, due to unknown or uncertain cause with the structural reactions manifest

VIII

Mental retardation due to uncertain (or presumed psychologic) cause with the functional reaction alone manifest:

Cultural-familial mental retardation

Psychogenic mental retardation associated with environmental deprivation (specify nature of deprivation)

Psychogenic mental retardation associated with emotional disturbance (specify)

Mental retardation associated with psychotic (or major personality) disorder (specify as, e.g., autism)

Mental retardation, other, due to uncertain cause with the functional reaction alone manifest

Diagnosis of the specific etiology is accomplished through standard medical diagnostic methodology, including a complete and accurate history of the disorder and a thorough investigation into the familial background of the patient. In addition to the general examination, a neurological examination, serological tests, urine tests, skull x-rays, spinal fluid examination, thyroid function tests, and air encephalography may be necessary diagnostic procedures. A knowledge of the principles of genetics is most helpful in evaluating the possible hereditary influences.

MANAGEMENT

In addition to the medical treatment dictated by the particular disorder, management involves a program of socialization which capitalizes on whatever potentialities the individual may have. Cases of moderate or severe mental retardation sometimes necessitate institutionalization of the individual, although the attitudes of the surrounding family members play a large role in determining what should or what must be done.

Training of the mentally retarded individual requires special skills, great patience, and kindness. This training can at times be best accomplished outside the home. Mentally retarded children are often happier when with other similarly limited children and protected from the demands of persons who are lacking in understanding. Counseling with family members is necessary.

A frequent reaction to the birth of a mentally retarded child is guilt or anger, sometimes projected to the other parent or to other relatives. The mentally retarded child may be the focus of parents' unexpressed anger toward each other. It is frequently difficult for parents to evaluate realistically the child's limitations; and the parents' attitudes toward the child may be highly irrational. Group therapy with parents of mentally retarded children offers support for the parents and helps parents adjust to the many difficulties these children present.

Tranquilizing drugs may be used to control the disturbed behavior which may occur with mental retardation. In spite of numerous overly optimistic accounts of gross increase in intellectual functioning accomplished with certain drugs, no medical treatment consistently improves intellectual functioning of mentally retarded individuals.

10 〰〰〰〰〰〰〰〰〰〰〰〰〰〰〰〰〰〰〰〰〰〰〰

Disorders of
Memory, Orientation,
and Consciousness

A difficult diagnostic problem frequently presented
to the physician involves the symptoms of disturbances of *memory,
orientation,* and *consciousness.*

Memory: *the general function of recalling or reproducing
acquired knowledge or experience.*
Orientation: *the general knowledge of who and where one
is and where one is going, both in time and place.*
Consciousness: *the general field of awareness in the sense of
knowing what is going on and what is being experienced.*

At times, it may be extremely difficult to determine whether disturbances in memory, orientation, or consciousness actually exist. These parameters are generally evaluated through verbal communication with the patient. For example, to evaluate a patient's orientation, such questions as the following are frequently used: "Who are you?" "Where do you live?" "What time is it?" "What is the date?" "Where are you now?" "What is the name of this place?" Thus, verbal communication becomes the object and the tool of the examination; but one's orientation is not really dependent upon the ability to tell about it. An individual in a catatonic stupor (a disorder described in Chapter 12) may be mute, make no response to questions, and stand in one position for hours; he may seem to be unresponsive and even "unconscious." However, when the episode is over, it may be revealed that in fact he knew very much about where he was, what was going on, and that he had a remarkable acuity of memory, although this was not being verbally transmitted.

A further complication in evaluating the possible presence of disturbances in memory, orientation, and consciousness is that one frequently has no previous measure with which the patient's present functioning can be compared. Thus, an individual of initially superior intelligence may have an impairment in memory and, nevertheless, still function as well as a person of average intelligence. Without any baseline with which to compare his present performance, it may be difficult to determine whether any impairment of functioning is actually present. Hence, disorders of memory, orientation, and consciousness are not always immediately obvious, and careful examination is required to ascertain their presence.

CLASSIFICATION

Assuming that disturbances in memory, orientation, and consciousness are present, the most important distinction is whether they are disturbances in brain cell function or structure ("organic") or generated on the basis of psychological, emotional causes ("functional" or "psychogenic").

ORGANIC DISORDERS

Disorders of memory, orientation, and consciousness are typically consistent with the primary symptoms of organic brain disorders. Consequently, this likelihood must always be carefully evaluated. Impairment of memory determined by pathological brain cell function or structure is generally most marked for recent events as opposed to past or remote experiences. The person may not recall what he had for breakfast but remembers many episodes of childhood. Memory difficulties may lead to compensatory fabrications ("confabulations") or to repetition of the same response ("perseveration").

Other intellectual functions are also impaired.[1] The ability to make verbal abstractions may be poor and reflect an extreme concreteness of thought. For instance, when asked "How are dog and lion alike?" the brain-damaged person may respond "They both have tails" or "They both have legs" rather than making a higher level abstraction, "They are animals." Arithmetic reasoning also is often impaired. The patient may appear confused and fail to recognize who or where he is. Such impairment in orientation is usually more marked for time than for place or person; he may fail to recognize the year, the month, or the day of the week. Social judgment may be impaired, and the emotional response is either extremely labile (laughing or crying inappropriately with sudden changes in response), or relatively unreactive.

Accompanying these primary signs of organic brain disorders, secondary signs arising from an exaggeration of the basic personality characteristics of the person may also occur; e.g., depression, anxiety, panic, paranoia, antisocial behavior. These associated reactions are not necessarily related in severity to the degree of the organic brain disorder or the extent of brain damage; rather they are more directly related to the patient's latent personality characteristics, his existing emotional conflicts, and the surrounding environmental influences. Nevertheless, these reactions may obscure the primary symptoms of

---

[1] For purposes of accurately determining the relative intellectual strengths and weaknesses, a formal intelligence test is mandatory. The best-known individual test in clinical practice is the Wechsler Adult Intelligence Scale (see Appendix).

a brain disorder and thus complicate diagnosis as well as management.

FUNCTIONAL DISORDERS

Although typically considered primary symptoms of organic brain disorders, disturbances of memory, orientation, and consciousness may have an emotional etiology. The major psychic mechanism involved is *dissociation,* a process closely allied with repression.

Dissociation: *the separation or splitting off of a segment of the personality in such a way that conscious awareness is not maintained.*

In dissociation, a group of psychological activities may lose its relationship with the rest of the personality and function more or less independently, separated from normal consciousness. Dissociation is purposive in that it permits the individual to discharge impulses in behavior which may be quite atypical for him, without the consequences of having to integrate or fuse the contrasting aspects or implications of this behavior into his total conscious awareness. Within relatively normal limits, this maneuver may be seen in the *compartmentalization* of the "Sunday saint and weekday sinner." In such reactions, it may seem as if the person has no awareness of the contrasting aspects of his behavior. The reaction is quite different from that of a normal person who may commit deeds which are not consistent with his moral standards, and from that in which the individual experiences guilt through an awareness of the discrepancy between his ideals and his behavior. In extreme compartmentalization, the patient may act as if two quite different people were involved, one not known to the other.

Of more abnormal significance is *amnesia,* a common dissociative reaction in which periods of time are simply blotted out of awareness. Amnesic material is usually that which would otherwise provoke either guilt or anxiety. The loss of memory may be very circumscribed in terms of time, place, or type of experience. Episodes of amnesia are frequently of sudden onset and, unlike the loss of mem-

)ccurs with organic brain dysfunction, there is usually a
rn of memory even though the loss may have continued
...₅ period of time.

Closely similar to dissociative amnesias, *dissociative fugue states*
involve a loss of memory which is associated with a physical flight.
During the episode of fugue, the person is driven by unconscious
impulses to perform complicated activities, frequently involving
changing his physical locations. Often these activities will be contrary to those which his conscience would normally permit him to
carry out. The fugue state may help the person escape from some
unpleasant or intolerable situation. After the termination of the
fugue, the patient may have a total amnesia for the events which
transpired, and perhaps awake to find himself in a strange city or
unusual circumstances.

> A forty-year-old amnesic male was brought to the ward of a
> general hospital, having been picked up in a daze by the police.
> He was unable to remember how he had left his home, although
> he had a vague recall that he had been befriended by a soldier
> at an Army base. Subsequent investigation revealed that while
> slightly intoxicated he had accompanied a soldier to an Army
> barracks and had ultimately been seduced into homosexual re-
> lations. Following a brief period of sleep, he simply "wandered
> off," and was later found fifty miles away.

Dissociation may be so complete and repetitive as to give rise to
a separately organized personality which functions outside the conscious control or awareness of the primary personality. This secondary personality, made up from normally repressed aspects of the
personality, is usually in striking contrast to the primary personality.
On some occasions, more than one body of normally dissociated
experiences may become independent, giving rise to more than one
secondary personality distinct from the others and from the primary
personality. This disorder is called *multiple personalities,* a phenomenon popularized in the book, *Three Faces of Eve.*[2]

> A striking example of multiple personality was also revealed in a
> patient hospitalized following a suicide attempt. Subsequent de-
> velopments revealed two distinct personalities: Martha (an ex-

[2] Thigpen, C. H., and Cleckley, H. M. New York: McGraw-Hill Book Company, Inc., 1957.

ceedingly conscientious mother and housewife who when depressed would attempt suicide, frequently by slashing her left wrist and arm) and Stella (a verbose woman who used alcohol excessively, swore profusely, and was exceedingly promiscuous). Although Stella knew of the existence of Martha, Martha did not know of Stella. Each had a relatively separate life, with different associations and contacts.

Altered states of consciousness may also occur in hysteria and schizophrenia. In "hysterical epilepsy," for instance, the loss of consciousness may appear similar to that occurring with organic epilepsy. Usually, however, the attacks occur in an emotional setting before an audience, with the patient rarely injuring himself during his "seizure." Schizophrenics may experience altered states of consciousness, with fluctuations in awareness being experienced passively without efforts at control.

Perhaps the most dramatic example of "functional" disorders of memory, orientation, and consciousness are those demonstrated in hypnosis. In this heightened state of suggestibility, the individual's memory, orientation, and consciousness may be manipulated to closely approximate conditions which occur as a result of brain damage. That these effects may likewise be easily removed by suggestion testifies to the purposive role these conditions may play, even when their appearance is deceptively like the effects of brain damage.

ETIOLOGY OF THE BRAIN DISORDERS

Brain disorders can arise on the basis of a wide variety of causative agents and lesions, including trauma, infections, intoxications, and nutritional as well as endocrine deficiencies. The severity of the mental syndrome is generally proportional to the extent of impairment of brain tissue function. The brain disorders are frequently separated into those that are "acute" and those that are "chronic," terms which refer primarily to the reversibility of brain pathology.

Acute brain disorders are those organic brain sydromes from which the patient recovers. Typical examples include those brain syndromes associated with intracranial infections (encephalitis, meningitis, and brain abscess); systemic infections (pneumonia, typhoid fever); drug or poison intoxication (barbiturates, bromides, opiates, lead, heavy metals); alcohol intoxication; trauma; circulatory disturbance (cerebral embolism, arterial hypertension); metabolic disturbance (uremia, diabetes, vitamin deficiency); and intracranial neoplasms. Any of these disorders, if sufficiently severe, can also lead to chronic irreversible damage.

Chronic brain disorders are those that result from irreversible impairment of conscious function. Although the underlying pathological process may partially subside, an irreducible minimum of brain tissue destruction remains, even though loss of function may be difficult to detect. Typical examples of chronic brain disorders include those brain syndromes associated with congenital cranial anomaly, central nervous system syphilis, intoxication, brain trauma, cerebral arteriosclerosis, embolism, hemorrhages, cardiovascular disease, senile brain disease, disturbances of metabolism and growth or nutrition, and intracranial neoplasm.

In addition to the mental status examination, the diagnosis of the etiology of either acute or chronic brain disorders may require extensive physical examination, including both routine and supplementary laboratory investigations: electroencephalogram, serological tests, skull x-rays, air encephalograms, ventriculography, angiography, etc. Careful inquiry must be made from reliable informants as to the patient's normal personality, previous history, and present physical and mental status.

PSYCHODYNAMICS AND PSYCHOGENESIS OF FUNCTIONAL DISTURBANCES OF MEMORY, ORIENTATION, AND CONSCIOUSNESS

The psychodynamics of functional disturbances of memory, orientation, and consciousness include the purposive nature of the episode, frequently used to blot out anxiety or guilt. Sometimes the episode serves as an escape for the patient from some situation, consciously or unconsciously viewed as intolerable or displeasing. Most authorities are impressed with the "hysterical" features of individuals who use dissociation extensively. These people often rely heavily on repression as a defense and remain extremely naive and uncritical in their thinking. Many show a tendency to engage in lying. Dissociative reactions are typically considered as neurotic disorders of the hysterical kind. Of recent recognition is the fact that the prior or accompanying mood of a dissociative reaction is frequently depression, a finding which has led some authorities to view dissociative reactions as akin to the shift that occurs in the manic-depressive cycles.

A frequent finding in those who experience dissociative reactions is that a model for such episodes has been established either by (1) a previous head injury or an amnesia occurring because of intoxication, or (2) identification with a significant person who may have experienced an amnesia or dissociative reaction of some kind. For example, an alcoholic parent may set a model by carrying out behavior while intoxicated in the presence of the child, behavior which is then denied or disowned by the simple explanation, "I didn't know what I was doing" (hence, "I am not responsible for what I did"). This kind of explanation serves to remove responsibility for the behavior as if it were some other person who had been involved. The patient who experiences dissociative reactions similarly has a defense which serves a self-excusing function.

Although documented cases of multiple personality are rare, it has appeared that an emotional trauma usually elicits the first utilization of massive dissociation.

> In the case described earlier, the patient's mother died when Martha was five years old. The mother had warned Martha that if she misbehaved, the mother would die. Two weeks following this warning, the mother did die and the patient felt responsible. The father was a brutal alcoholic. Later sent to a strict religious school, the patient was seduced by a religious leader at the age of eight, and on subsequent occasions was induced by him to perform other sexual activities. She was told that she would commit a mortal sin if she ever talked about this. Shortly thereafter, she began to be accused by teacher and classmates of improper behavior, such as telling dirty jokes, walking out of religious services, and refusing to follow the pattern of expected behavior. The patient would bitterly deny these accusations, not remembering herself as having done the things. During the early years of school, teachers pressured her to change to writing with her

right hand by telling her it was sinful to use her left hand, an experience apparently related to her later desire to cut this hand when depressed.

MANAGEMENT

BRAIN DISORDERS

Forms of medical treatment must be directed toward the specific brain syndrome. Apart from the medical treatment indicated, the most important aspect of management, particularly with the chronic irreversible brain disorders, is adequate placement of the patient in the most appropriate setting for his care and protection. With the extended life span, senile and arteriosclerotic changes result in increasing numbers of geriatric patients who often cannot be cared for at home. Unfortunately, ideal settings for such patients are seldom available, and they frequently must be placed in overly crowded mental hospitals not suitable for their care.

FUNCTIONAL DISORDERS

Treatment of the personality disturbances in which dissociative reactions occur generally requires extensive psychotherapy. Nevertheless, in the immediate situation, the physician may be able to provide support and reassurance to the patient and his family. The fear of what he may have done may cause the patient to perpetuate the amnesia. This fear may also give rise to a state of panic. Through the use of amytal sodium or pentothal sodium, it is sometimes helpful to try to reconstruct what in effect did happen. Reconstruction is done gradually, eliciting a methodical, painstaking recall of the episode which has been "blacked out." Hypnosis is also available as a means of reconstructing what happened during the amnesic period.

11 ∿∿∿∿∿∿∿∿∿∿∿∿∿∿∿∿∿∿∿∿∿∿∿∿∿∿∿∿∿∿∿∿∿

Paranoid

Conditions

In some instances, the patient's complaint or symptom will be a distortion in thinking which is characterized as a *delusion.*

Delusion: *a serious disorder in judgment, represented by the maintenance of a false belief, idea, or set of ideas not consistent with reality and not susceptible to the influence of reason, logic, common sense, persuasion, or rational explanation.*

Although many people hold ideas which perhaps are not supported by fact, these ideas are generally common in the culture or subculture in which they live. A delusion, on the other hand, is a highly personalized distortion of reality, motivated by greatly personalized needs. Since the term is generally applied only to ideas which reflect gross distortion of reality, a delusion is typically considered the hallmark of a psychosis.

CLASSIFICATION

Delusions may be *systematized* into highly developed and rationalized schemes which have a high degree of internal consistency once the basic premise is granted; or they may be *unsystematized* in the sense of their being less organized and lacking in internal consistency. The persistence of an unchanging delusional system is the outstanding characteristic of those disorders labeled "paranoid" or "paranoia." A distinction is sometimes made in terms of the degree of personality disorganization which occurs with the delusional beliefs.

In *paranoia*, the delusion is a relatively isolated symptom in which the personality otherwise appears intact. The delusion frequently may appear logical, although exceedingly intricate and complex. In *paranoid states*, on the other hand, the delusion is less systematized and elaborate, although the personality does not otherwise show obvious indication of deterioration or regression. In *paranoid schizophrenia*, however, the basic disorder is schizophrenia with delusions appearing as one aspect of a more general personality disorganization. The delusions may be highly implausible and extremely bizarre.

Paranoid delusions are generally classified as to their content:

Delusions of persecution in which the person holds the false belief that others are out to harm him or destroy him in some way.

Delusions of reference in which the person inappropriately feels that others are looking at him or talking about him.

Delusions of grandeur in which the person magnifies his own importance in a totally unrealistic fashion, believing himself to be an important, influential figure, e.g., Napoleon, God, Franklin Roosevelt.

Body delusions in which the person holds grossly bizarre ideas about his body, represented by such beliefs as that his body is rotting, changing its sex, or emitting foul odors.

Delusions of influence in which the person inappropriately believes he is being influenced against his will by means which usually are not consistent with reality as known by others.

Sometimes, in a complex delusional system, many or all of these features are found.

> A twenty-three-year-old schizophrenic man felt that he was being turned at various times into a wild animal, a baby, and a woman. He had thoughts that he saw the devil and that he himself was God. He had the idea that his penis was shrinking into his body, that it would disappear and he would be "turned into a woman." He felt that electricity was passing through him, and that little white, round bugs and brown bugs "like little sticks" were coming out of his body. He imagined that control was being taken of his body, that he had been hypnotized and was to be used for experiments. At various times, he felt he would have to make a choice about "something that could go either way," a conflict sometimes expressed in terms of whether he would be a man or a woman; at other times, he saw a circle and a square, feeling he had to decide if he were going to be one or the other. The patient kept voluminous notes on all his reactions. Many of them reflected his underlying confusion about his own identity: "I wonder what everyone thinks I am—a criminal, an animal from the woods, or a crazy insane person, or a queer, or a killer, a murderer, or a thief, or waiting to break in someone's house and grab a girl or a woman and rape her and make her perform immoral acts?"

The bizarre, illogical, and unsystematized nature of this delusional belief is consistent with paranoid schizophrenia. Because most paranoid manifestations occur in settings characteristic of either schizophrenia or some other disorder (manic-depressive, involutional, or a sociopathic disturbance), some authorities would challenge the existence of "paranoia" as a distinct entity. Nevertheless, in view of what often appears to be their specific underlying psychodynamics, paranoid conditions shall be dealt with separately.

PSYCHODYNAMICS

In paranoid delusions, there are generally both suspicious and grandiose features, although one or the other may predominate. In all delusions, the assumption, at least implicit, is that the person who has the delusion feels he is a very important person. Consequently, it is not difficult to understand that delusions frequently are related to problems centering around self-esteem, prestige, and autonomy.

The primary defense mechanism in handling the anxiety precipitated by the conflict leading to a paranoid delusion is *projection*.

Projection: *the unconscious process by which emotionally unacceptable impulses are rejected and attributed to (projected onto) others.*

Within limits, projection is a defense used by everyone as a way of excusing oneself for his own faults and shortcomings; it is easy to shift the responsibility from oneself to some external person, object, or event. Nevertheless, in paranoia the boundary between fantasy and external reality becomes blurred to the point where thinking and perceiving may be autistic, illogical, egocentric, and magical, rather than more or less reality-oriented, organized, and logical.

The traditional dynamics of paranoid delusions were stated by Freud in his classic paper, "Psychoanalytic Notes on an Autobiographical Account of a Case of Paranoia." In this paper, Freud analyzed the case of Dr. Daniel Schreber, a famous jurist, who has been referred to as psychiatry's most famous and frequently quoted patient. Schreber had written an autobiographical account of his illness, "Memoirs of My Nervous Illness," in the years 1900–1902. In 1910, the memoirs came to Freud's attention, and a year later he published his celebrated paper, an analysis based on the text of the memoirs.

Schreber was the third of five children. His father was an eminent physician who developed and published a system of therapeutic gymnastics. At age 36, Schreber married a woman 15 years younger than he. His wife was diabetic, and the marriage resulted in six full-term stillbirths. Schreber's first illness began at the age of 42 when he developed a severe hypochondriasis of eight months' duration. In 1893, nine years later, he developed his second mental illness, leading to confinement from 1893 to 1902. This illness also began with hypochondriasis, although other symptoms soon appeared. In the course of this illness, he displayed mutism, stupor, impulsiveness, suicidal attempts, hallucinations, delusions of persecution, ideas of miracles being performed upon his body, insomnia, compulsive bellowing, obsessive thinking, and transvestism. It has been said that he manifested all the symptoms of psychopathology at one time or another. Following an acute phase, his illness crystallized into the paranoid delusion that he was gradually becoming unmanned so that "by divine fertilization, offspring will issue from my lap."

Using the material in the memoirs for illustrative purposes, Freud proposed the theory that paranoid delusions represent a denial of unconscious homosexual impulses. In his analysis of Schreber's autobiography, Freud explained various forms of paranoia as exhausting the ways in which the proposition "I [a man] love him" can be denied:

Persecution: I do not *love* him. I *hate* him. I hate him because he persecutes me.

Erotomania: I do not love *him.* I love *her,* which (in accordance with the need for projection) is changed to: I notice that *she* loves me.

Jealousy: I do not love him. *She* loves him.

Another kind of contradiction is possible in which the whole proposition is denied: "I do not love at all. I do not love anyone" becomes the equivalent of "I love only myself" and forms the basis of *megalomania.*

Since Freud's inferences regarding the psychodynamics of paranoia, the relationship between paranoia and homosexual impulses has been brought into question by cases which do not appear to reflect any homosexual problem. Inasmuch as the unacceptable impulses are unconscious, however, the fact that they are not discernible in the patient's overt behavior cannot be taken as evidence that disproves Freud's hypothesis. Likewise, some cases show both paranoia and overt homosexuality, a finding which is taken by other authorities as also disproving Freud's theory, since paranoia presumably represents a denial of homosexuality. The coexistence of both paranoia and overt homosexuality is likewise not contrary to the traditional theory, since the homosexuality which reaches expression in overt behavior need not bear a direct relationship to the homosexual impulses which are being denied and projected from the unconscious. For example, although a patient may engage in fairly conventional homosexual practices, he may have to resort to psychotic defenses against more unconscious and totally unacceptable sadistic and incorporative impulses.

Regardless of the role that homosexual impulses may play in the specific dynamics of a particular paranoid patient, the role of hostile impulses is crucial. In fact, many authorities believe that underlying homosexual love must be defended against by the patient, not because of the social disapproval of homosexuality, per se, but because the homosexual love is fused with tremendously hostile impulses which are perceived by the patient as threatening the welfare of both himself and the object of the homosexual love.

The precipitating factors of an overt paranoid episode often involve situations in which the patient's security is threatened, either through competition, rebuff, humiliation, or defeat. Since submission is often equated in our culture with playing the passive, feminine role, homosexual anxieties are often precipitated by conditions which are more directly related to power, assertion, and dependency than to any immediate sexual motivation.

A further contribution of Freud to understanding the psychodynamics of paranoia was his recognition that the projection, perhaps in a manner not immediately apparent, may incorporate a "nucleus" or "kernel" of truth, i.e., that the projection is instigated by something or someone whose impulses or qualities meet it part way. Thus, projections are not made upon a "blank screen" entirely without realistic foundations, although they are grossly exaggerated.

Evidence of the nucleus of truth in Schreber's delusions is provided by the recent revelations (see Neiderland) that Schreber's father used extremely sadistic devices on his children as part of his advocated method of child rearing. Many of the somatic reactions experienced in Schreber's delusions bear a close relationship to the experiences he had as a child. A crucial adult relationship for Schreber was that with his physician, Dr. Paul Emil Fleschig, who appears to have been a representation of Schreber's father.

PSYCHOGENESIS

The etiology of paranoid reactions is unknown, with theories ranging from that of a gene-controlled, constitutional defect to that of damaging early life experiences occurring at a rather specific stage in the child's development.

Persons who develop paranoid reactions have frequently been excessively secretive and seclusive throughout life, evidencing only minimal capacity to trust other people. Their ability to view others realistically is often disturbed. They often misinterpret the actions and motives of others. They are frequently extremely sensitive and rigid, guarding what they perceive as their "rights" with absolute literal interpretation of the rules, resorting to constant bickering when the absolute interpretation is not achieved.

The use of projection is especially prominent in the small child who naturally attributes his own feelings and impulses to other people, animals, and objects. Children's stories often perpetuate the idea that animals and inanimate objects "feel" just as they do. Parental comments such as "the nasty, old floor" when the child falls, facilitate the establishment of a defense pattern in which one's own responsibility is diminished and blame is displaced.

There is some evidence that the crucial time at which the basis for pathological projection becomes established is in the earliest phases of habit training (the so-called "early anal stage" of development). The physical act of defecation and the expulsion of unwanted body contents are believed by some authorities to set the model for the later handling of unwanted mental contents through analogous expulsion. It is at this time that the pressure placed on the child provokes a struggle which centers around autonomy versus shame and self-doubt. It is also at this time that the child becomes aware of having a "behind" which he cannot see yet which is dominated by stronger people and forces. (Fears of being attacked from behind, of "anal rape," of being used for ulterior motives, of being controlled by unseen influences frequently constitute crucial aspects of paranoia.) [1] In the process of bowel training, parents often use particularly humiliating, punitive, and even sadistic threats, methods, and devices. Although some authorities would debate the invariability of a relationship between habit training and adult paranoia, most people agree that paranoid adults have been subjected in their early childhood to unusual hostility as well as deception and deceit, a condition which contributes to their later perception of the world around them.

> In the case of the twenty-three-year-old paranoid schizophrenic patient reported earlier, investigation revealed an extremely punitive stepfather who frequently beat the patient. The mother, while stating that she was concerned because often there was blood on the bathroom floor, gave no evidence that she ever tried to interfere with her husband's treatment of the boy. It was later revealed by the mother's sister that the mother herself had been promiscuous throughout married life, had mistreated the boy from birth, and had later used the boy in her practiced deceptions involving lovers while her husband was at work.

SUMMARY

The following assumptions are helpful in understanding delusions and paranoid conditions:

1. A delusion, as a serious distortion of reality, is typically considered indicative of a psychosis.

---

[1] Although paranoid delusions are less frequently expressed in predominantly *oral* terms, some authorities nevertheless feel that *oral ejection* (vomiting or spitting out) in the infant becomes the model for projection, rather than *anal expulsion* serving as the prototype.

2. Delusions are frequently related to problems centering about self-esteem, prestige, and autonomy.

3. The primary defense mechanism operating in a delusion is projection, often as a means of handling unacceptable homosexual impulses.

4. Projection is a defense used by everyone on occasion; in paranoia, however, it reaches pathological proportions with a loss of ability to distinguish reality from fantasy.

5. The early model for projection may be established in early life, particularly in relation to habit (toilet) training.

6. Persons who become paranoid frequently have a childhood history of extremely harsh, cruel, or brutal treatment.

MANAGEMENT

Since the primary characteristic of a delusion is its invulnerability to the influence of external persuasion or logic, it is obvious that nothing usually can be gained by trying to convince the patient of the illogicality of his delusional belief. Such an attempt may only intensify the patient's anxiety and increase the need for further projection.

Because such a patient is often extraordinarily perceptive at recognizing insincerity and trickery, it is generally desirable to be honest and straightforward, without necessarily actually accepting or challenging the reality of the delusional belief. Inasmuch as the maintenance of a delusional belief may constitute a danger to the patient as well as to others who are the target of the patient's hostility, it is often necessary that such patients be hospitalized.

Drugs frequently may be utilized with success in diminishing the anxiety which precipitates the formation of a delusion. On some occasions, removing the individual from the stressful environment will in itself bring about an improvement. Although psychotherapy may be extremely difficult to initiate when the individual is acutely paranoid, the ultimate resolution of the patient's difficulties in perceiving others can come about only through the corrective influence of a long-term psychotherapeutic relationship with a therapist. He must be one whom the patient can trust, can use as a target for projection without fear of retaliation, can use as a model for identification, and with whom he can establish a more adequate empathic delineation of ego boundaries.

12

Schizophrenia

Not necessarily related to the complaints directly reported by the patient, the manifestations of this serious personality disorganization may be expressed on levels of functioning which, only through the observer's abstraction, are ultimately labeled "*schizophrenia*" or "*schizophrenic.*"

Schizophrenia: *A severe personality disorganization, at times manifesting psychotic symptoms, predicated upon an underlying defect in reality testing which may be only subtly detectable. Typical characteristics include (1) major distortions in thinking, (2) disturbances in affect, (3) disturbances in ego boundaries, (4) difficulties in interpersonal relation-*

> *ships, basic to which may be chronic impairment of the ca-*
> *pacity to experience pleasure.*[1]

The complex phenomena which may be indicative of schizophrenia can usually be subsumed in these four areas:

1. DISTORTIONS IN THINKING

One of the signs traditionally considered pathognomic of schizophrenia is a breakdown and disorganization of the patient's thought processes. The ordinary rules of logic do not hold; rather, thinking is much more like that of the child or of a dreamlike state. Thinking may be autistic, condensed, highly symbolic, and bizarre. Illogical associations, clang associations, or "word salad" may prevail in speech. The capacity to make verbal abstractions may be deficient. There may be either a dearth of ideas and a slowing of the thought processes or an overproductivity of ideas. In mild form, an underlying thinking disorder may be difficult to recognize and may be expressed in an associative dyscontrol, evident only when the individual becomes anxious or is placed in a stressful situation. In its most obvious form, the thinking disorder may be expressed in *delusions* (fixed ideas not influenced by reason or rational explanation) and *hallucinations* (sensory experiences occurring without an external realistic perceptual stimulus).

2. DISTURBANCES IN AFFECT

The term "schizophrenia" typically implies a "split" between the affective life and the ideational life of the individual, i.e., affect and feeling are not in harmony with the thought being experienced.[2]

---

[1] While most authorities would agree on the relevance of these four characteristics for the diagnosis of schizophrenia, there is less agreement as to what are primary and what are secondary manifestations of the disorder. For example, some authorities consider anhedonia or a pleasure deficiency as a basic defect in individuals who are schizophrenic. Other authorities would view the observable pleasure deficiency in the schizophrenic to be a logical reaction to his other difficulties, more basic to which may be the disorder in thinking.

[2] Literal interpretation of the concept "split personality" has led to the popular but somewhat inaccurate conception of a schizophrenic as someone who

Typical responses to emotional stimuli may reflect *inappropriate affect* (such as smiling while discussing a sad event), *blandness of affect* (apathy, aloofness, and dreaminess), or *rigidity of affect* (stereotyped emotional patterns regardless of the external stimulus).

3. DISTURBANCES IN EGO BOUNDARIES

The schizophrenic has great difficulty in differentiating stimuli from within or without the body, reality from fantasy, his own thoughts from those of others—in short, where, in a sense, he leaves off and outer reality begins.[3] (See pages 17, 50.) The absence of a firm sense of self-identity or ego boundaries is considered the basic disturbance in schizophrenia by some authorities. Whether a primary or secondary phenomenon, however, disturbances in this area underlie the difficulty which schizophrenics frequently have in properly evaluating or testing reality.

4. DIFFICULTIES IN INTERPERSONAL RELATIONSHIPS

The inability to establish satisfactory interpersonal relationships is often considered one of the basic indications of a schizophrenic process. Marked *ambivalence* generally characterizes all aspects of the schizophrenic's daily life, often with accompanying difficulty around the appropriate expression and modulation of hostile impulses. *Anhedonia* (a chronic defect in pleasure capacity), accompanied by inordinate social fear, distrust, and expectation of rejection, is present to a degree not generally found in other disorders.

---

somehow feels or acts as if he were two different people. If at all relevant, this conception is more akin to the disorder "multiple personality," than to schizophrenia, per se. The "split" in schizophrenia refers to the discrepancy between thinking and feeling.

[3] In normal life, such dissolution of ego boundaries is most closely approximated in the dream state, wherein the world may seem to disappear and the boundaries between the self and others and between reality and fantasy are most fluid. For example, in a dream, one may be at once watching something that is being done while also being the one doing it. In certain phases of schizophrenia, it is as if the dream were continued over into the waking state. The feelings which such a state may precipitate are similar to the brief panic which may occur in a normal person unable to arouse himself completely from a frightening dream.

CLASSIFICATION

In its grossest forms, the schizophrenic disorder manifests symptoms which are easy to recognize and identify. These symptoms may be acute, chronic, or intermittent in appearance. In some instances, a presumed "normal" individual may demonstrate a rather sudden eruption of blatant schizophrenic symptoms. In other instances, the symptoms are persistent and chronic. In phases of relative clinical muteness, schizophrenia may be difficult to recognize. Nevertheless, most authorities conceive of schizophrenia as a chronic disorder in which only the overt clinical manifestations evidence much change throughout life.

PROCESS VS. REACTIVE SCHIZOPHRENIA

To some authorities, the most important differentiation of those patients called "schizophrenic" is between those individuals in whom the onset of the disorder has been early but slow and insidious, usually without apparent external precipitating causes, and usually of poor prognosis (process schizophrenia), and those in which the onset has been more rapid, frequently precipitated by some stressful event in later life, and usually of fairly good prognosis (reactive schizophrenia). Several terms have been used to distinguish between these two extreme groups: dementia praecox versus schizophrenia, typical versus atypical, and schizophrenic versus schizophreniform psychoses. Although this distinction cuts across the traditional classifications of schizophrenia, the process type would come closer to the *simple* and *hebephrenic* forms; the reactive type would come closer to the *catatonic* and *paranoid* forms.

SIMPLE SCHIZOPHRENIA

This is characterized by apathy, indifference, withdrawal, and lack of ambition. Other than the extreme disturbances in interest and activity, there are frequently no gross evidences of distortions of reality. Many chronic "drifters" and "ne'er do wells" may be of this type. In some instances, indifference and irresponsibility lead to difficulty with the law. The onset for this type of disturbance is frequently in early adolescence, at the time the individual is faced with the necessity for making the transition from childhood to adult heterosexual and social adjustment with its concomitant bearing of responsibility.

HEBEPHRENIC TYPE

This may be characterized by extreme silliness and inappropriateness of behavior. The onset of this disorder is usually insidious and early, frequently around adolescence. The ultimate disintegration of personality is generally greater than in any other form of schizophrenia. Delusions and hallucinations may be present and are frequently extremely bizarre. Speech and behavioral disturbances are common.

CATATONIC TYPE

This type has motor symptoms which are prominent, either of stupor or overactivity; negativism, oppositional behavior, and automatisms are outstanding features. Frequently the patient will maintain states of physical immobility for long periods. Disorganized overactivity may also be found, either uncontrollable excitement or disorganized motor activity. The appearance of these symptoms is usually sudden; prognosis for a single attack is somewhat favorable.

PARANOID TYPE

This type has delusions of persecution or grandiosity which are prominent (see Chapter 11). Onset is frequently later in life than the other forms of schizophrenia and is often ushered in by a period of marked hypochondriacal complaints. In general, there is less personality disorganization and deterioration in paranoid schizophrenia than in the other forms; consequently, many types of paranoid schizophrenia go undetected in our society.

PSEUDONEUROTIC TYPE

In this, the basic psychotic process is marked by numerous seemingly neurotic symptoms and a pervasive anxiety. There are usually numerous hysterical and obsessive-compulsive symptoms which, in themselves, might each appear to be neurotic rather than psychotic. Nevertheless, upon close inspection, the more typical disturbances of schizophrenia will be found. A chaotic sexuality is also frequently present.

SCHIZO-AFFECTIVE PSYCHOSIS

With this type manic-depressive features coexist with typically schizophrenic ones. The mood may be of elation, depression, or both. In spite of the marked affective features, the patient's behavior and thought processes may also be so bizarre that they are obviously schizophrenic. Consistent with disorders that show prominent affective features, prognosis for any single attack is generally considered favorable.

LATENT SCHIZOPHRENIA

This is a form of schizophrenia not directly manifested in behavior but indicating a potentiality for decompensation into an overt schizophrenic state.

The schizophrenic disorders do not, in all instances, exist in the pure types suggested by the traditional classification of paranoid, catatonic, simple, and hebephrenic. In some instances, the patient will manifest symptoms of various types over a period of time. This is particularly true of patients who at first appear as paranoid or catatonic and later regress to the simple or hebephrenic stages. For this reason, some authorities prefer thinking of the various forms of schizophrenia as typical courses of events rather than as different types of the disorder.

PSYCHODYNAMICS

As previously indicated, overt schizophrenic symptoms may develop slowly over a period of time, without evidence of any discernible precipitating factor. A progressive deterioration of previously established habits may be recognized only in perspective, thus making it extremely difficult to determine just when the onset began. In other instances, the onset of overt symptoms may be dramatic and sudden, often occurring in response to a clearly discernible stress. Prognosis in the latter instance is generally much more favorable in terms of a probable return to a productive level of premorbid functioning.

The acute outbreak of specific schizophrenic symptoms usually follows a frustrating experience or a situation in some way perceived as stressful. At such a time, there may be a sporadic appearance of marked obsessive, depressive, or hysterical symptoms by which it seems that neurotic defenses are being used to bind or control the anxiety evoked by the threat. In this prodromal period, there may be marked fluctuation of these symptoms within a relatively brief period. The ushering in of frank schizophrenic symptoms may then be perceived as a manifestation of *regression*.[4]

Regression: *a return or withdrawal to earlier established modes of functioning. Although present in some degree in many psychogenic disorders, regression in schizophrenia is more pervasive, often to the preverbal period of development when ego boundaries were not clearly differentiated, reality-testing ability was not well established, and thinking was primitive and prelogical.*

To be sure, such regression is never total or complete; characteristic of the schizophrenic are the marked unevenness of the regression

---

[4] Most authorities conceive of regression as a defense against anxiety or threat, similar to other defenses such as projection, repression, denial, etc. On the other hand, there are some who view regression as of a somewhat different order, regression representing the ultimate threat against which all other defenses are utilized.

and the resulting disorganization of personality. Even in the extreme form of catatonic withdrawal, the person still maintains some contact with the world about him. The fact that relatedness to other people is never totally excluded makes it possible for meaningful interpersonal contact to occur in even the most regressed or withdrawn patient.

A period at which such withdrawal or regression is common is at the time the individual is faced with the task of completing the transition from adolescence to maturity. The necessary social and heterosexual adjustments expected at this time may present a hurdle which cannot be successfully overcome by individuals whose basic ego integrity has not been securely attained previously. Sexual intimacy, particularly as experienced in the impulse to merge with another person and the threat to one's own autonomy in so doing, may be especially threatening. At this time, one's sense of personal identity is in constant flux, repeatedly being gained and lost due to radical body changes. These changes are made even more acute because of adult reactions. One has the appearance of an adult, yet is not emotionally an adult. Concurrently, our culture pressures the adolescent to make an occupational choice and a commitment to the competition which this occupational choice entails.

Stresses of later life may also strain a previous adjustment. Occupational success or failure, marriage, parenthood, illness, disillusionment over life's failures, actual or anticipated death of parents, diminishing sexual prowess, or any vicissitude of life may create a disequilibrium which makes prior effective defenses inadequate. In some instances, a threat which appears minimal can apparently trigger off a catastrophic regression; in other instances, the threat may be great.

Those who view schizophrenia as essentially a disorder of interpersonal relationships stress the ways in which the schizophrenic reacts to other people and the anxiety these interactions evoke. Feelings of rejection and an intolerable lack of self-respect frequently are prominent in the schizophrenic. Withdrawal from emotional involvement with other people is often an outstanding feature. While relationships may be highly ambivalent (i.e., fused with both love and hate), the person has great difficulty in properly modulating and appropriately expressing his resentment and anger. Frequently his dependency on other people is so great that he cannot risk their rejection by fully expressing his actual feelings. An underlying fear of his own hostility, perceived as being so great that it might lead to murder, frequently keeps the schizophrenic from any expressions of aggression or love. At times, fear of retaliation for his own murderous rage or his improper thoughts will motivate regression into a state of withdrawal, complete passivity, or panic. Relating to others is also complicated by the schizophrenic's confused sexual identity, making a mature heterosexual adjustment difficult. In some instances, sexual intimacy, either homosexual or heterosexual, is emotionally painful; in other instances, sexual acting-out may occur chaotically.

In a real sense, the schizophrenic often does not know who he is—male or female, human or nonhuman, fully alive or partially dead. Feeling isolated and rejected, he acts in such a way as to elicit rejection from others, a response which serves to confirm his basic view of himself. Heterosexual peers are often viewed primarily as sources of dependency gratification; offspring are viewed either as competitors or as self-extensions. Sharing and intimacy may be difficult, eliciting anxiety which only leads to further isolation and withdrawal.

PSYCHOGENESIS

There is no common agreement about the etiology of the schizophrenic disorders. Major theories pertaining to its genesis include both organic and psychological determinants.

GENETIC INFLUENCES

Many authorities consider schizophrenia essentially an inherited disorder which is either present or absent in any individual, while allowing that life stress may determine whether clinical evidence of the disorder ever develops. Genetic studies have shown a remarkable concordance of the disorder in identical twins, as opposed to decreasing expectancy rates in nonidentical twins, siblings, and half-siblings (in that order). A trend discernible in the field in recent years would perhaps be an increasing agreement that a predisposition to develop schizophrenia may be inherited. The most persistent finding in studies of the families of schizophrenics is the serious disturbance in the family environment. To date, specific genetic determinants have yet to be isolated.

PHYSIOLOGICAL INFLUENCES

Various theories on the etiology of schizophrenia have proposed physiological factors related to (1) constitutional physique, (2) the endocrine glands, (3) the cardiovascular system, and (4) brain functioning. Many studies have reported the discovery of important biochemical variations from normal in persons who are schizophrenic. Nevertheless, such results generally have either not been confirmed or, where confirmed, are not sufficient to account fully for the disorder. Many studies have not been controlled for physical activity, food-intake, or other important variables. When one recognizes that body chemistry can be altered significantly merely by rate of breathing, it is not surprising to discover that grossly disturbed patients show physiological changes not found in the nonschizophrenic person. However, any causal link between such changes and the disorder has yet to be conclusively proved. Taking a lead from the lack of pleasure capacity in schizophrenics, some authorities assume that brain dysfunction is basic, finding support for this view in studies which show that electrical stimulation of the limbic system in the brain gives rise to a sensation which is interpreted as pleasurable. However, since anhedonia as experienced by schizophrenics is mainly involved with interpersonal rather than noninterpersonal pursuits, other authorities assume the etiology is primarily interpersonal (psychological).

PSYCHOLOGICAL FACTORS

Major psychological theories about the genesis of schizophrenia concern the importance of early interpersonal relationships, particularly those with the mothering person. When one recognizes the

extreme helplessness and dependency of the newborn, it is not surprising that a high potential for psychopathy exists when the developing child must pass from a state of complete symbiosis with
the mother to that of a differentiated, independently functioning
individual. The rapid changes occurring in the child himself during
this critical period of development complicate the learning situation
for both mother and child.

An essential aspect of early learning is that subsumed in the concept of "developing ego boundaries" or "a firm sense of self-aware-
ness and self-identity." The relationship between self and one's bodily urges, distinguished from the other aspects of reality, can become
increasingly differentiated only when the mothering environment
provides consistent support and definition of the child's own auton-
omous contribution. Even the mere act of handling the baby in the
course of feeding and care may help on a tactile basis to establish
a clearly defined body-image. If such mothering is lacking or incon-
sistent, a firm sense of reality with appropriate differentiation between self and nonself may actually never develop. Also, at this time,
a sense of trust is established with the mothering figure, a relationship which sets the prototype for all future relationships.

The woman who has been described as the kind of mother who
makes schizophrenic development likely has been called the "schizophrenogenic mother." She has been labeled variously as "hostile,"
"rejecting," "overprotective," "sadistically critical," "anxious,"
"cold," "distant," and "unable to respond warmly to the child as
other than an extension of herself," characteristics, incidentally, not
confined to schizophrenic families. Family studies have indicated a
high degree of marital discord frequently correlated with the occurrence of schizophrenia. While no one constellation has been proven
specific for the familes of schizophrenics which is not found in nonschizophrenic families, the intensity of the conflict, tension, and
anxiety found in the former frequently makes it tempting to infer
a causal relationship between such a condition and the development
of the disorder.

In view of the outstanding role of distorted thought processes in
schizophrenia, it is not surprising that disturbances in communication between members of the family have also been incriminated

as fostering the development of the disorder. A typical disturbance noted in schizophrenic families is a discrepancy between the parents' verbal remarks and their behavior, perpetuated in such a way that the child has difficulty either discriminating properly or seeking clarification of such discrepancies, since he senses either would be a threat to the security of his relationship with the needed parent. In some instances, the child may be unable to predict the attitude of a given parent on any given occasion with any degree of consistency. Other studies have suggested that such families frequently conjointly practice a deception in relation to some painful family reality, as though they were tacitly agreeing that they will act as if neither the reality nor the denial of it were so. In some instances, the model presented to children by the parents directly perpetuates excessive use of denial and projection, particularly when destructive or sexual assaults on the child must then be denied or repressed by the child as the only means of maintaining his relationship with the parent. There is some evidence that such early trauma which was originally repressed may, in the later schizophrenic episode, be included in the delusional ideation, i.e., that the delusion may in fact represent the recall and elaboration (reminiscent recapitulation) of an earlier repressed experience.

> It will be recalled that in the classic case of Schreber (Chapter 11), the patient believed that miracles were being performed on his body. Such delusions appeared not to have any plausible explanation. Nevertheless, the reality basis for these delusions has become indicated through the discovery that the father had utilized an array of orthopedic devices on his son, which procedures were obvious precursors of Schreber's later delusions. The meaning of Schreber's difficulties involving mysterious "little men" a few millimeters tall and his "plurality of heads" can be related to the drawings of little human figures depicting a variety of gymnastic exercises, used to illustrate the father's writings. (See Niederland.)

The most plausible etiological view is that there is no single cause for the diverse symptoms which are subsumed in the label "schizophrenia." It appears that a complex interplay of both biological and social forces are at work, perhaps to varying degrees in the diverse aspects of the syndrome. It is also reasonable to presume that the ultimate understanding will reveal that that which is now considered to be a single disorder is actually a number of different entities. The distinction between process and reaction schizophrenia, for example, is accepted by some authorities as a representation of disorders with quite different etiologies; i.e., that somatogenic or organic factors are crucial in the development of process schizophrenia, while psychogenic factors are responsible for the development of reactive schizophrenia.

SUMMARY

The following assumptions are helpful in understanding schizophrenia:

1. The etiology of schizophrenia is essentially unknown. It is reasonable to assume, however, that there is no single cause for the diverse symptoms given the label "schizophrenia."

2. Typical characteristics of schizophrenia include: distortions in thinking, disturbances in affect, disturbances in body-ego boundaries, and difficulties in interpersonal relationships.

3. Although traditional diagnosis differentiates four primary types (simple, hebephrenic, paranoid, and catatonic), the schizophrenic disorders do not, in all instances, conform to such classification. In schizophrenia, the symptomatology may be highly kaleidoscopic, changing within relatively brief periods.

4. Prognosis is generally much more favorable when the onset of the disorder is sudden and has discernible precipitating factors. The contrast of such reactions with those that have a slow, insidious onset, without discernible precipitating factors, have led some authorities to conclude that at least two different syndromes may be involved.

5. Ultimate clarification of these disturbances may reveal a variety of disorders in which both biological and social forces vary in degree and kind.

MANAGEMENT

A major consideration in managing the schizophrenic patient is whether he is a danger to himself or to other people so that hospitalization is necessary. Many schizophrenics are able to work and perform normal activities, and concurrently can be carried in psychotherapy designed to support their defenses and widen their effective contact with reality.

With the advent of modern tranquilizing drugs, great numbers of schizophrenic patients who previously would necessarily have been committed to hospitals are now able to function outside a hospital setting. In fact, the first major breakthrough in the problem of the increasing hospital population has occurred as a result of these drugs. It is generally recognized, however, that in no sense are present drugs a cure for schizophrenia. In common with other physical methods of treating the disorder (including electroconvulsive therapy, insulin coma therapy, and various forms of brain surgery), the newer drugs appear to help diminish anxiety and reaction to stress by decreasing the individual's response potential. Although empirical evidence clearly indicates that many of these treatments work in the sense of relieving symptoms, a thorough understanding of how they work has not yet been attained.

Recent years have brought increasing optimism regarding results of psychotherapeutic intervention with schizophrenic patients, even some of those who previously would have been considered inaccessible to any form of treatment. Nevertheless, even the most enthusiastic psychotherapists would not claim that successful treatment will completely cure the disorder. The goal is generally increased social adaptation, with a relief of incapacitating symptoms (social recovery).

Concomitant with increasing optimism in relation to treatment, increasing acceptance and tolerance for mental illness have made it possible to give much greater freedom to patients who previously might have had to be protected from society's rejection and hostility. The "open-door" policy, a trend begun in England with the goal of making mental hospitals much more like general medical hospitals, is being extended to hospital wards which at one time enforced a marked restriction on patients' activities and liberties. Much greater understanding has also been gained regarding the extent to which patients live up to the role in which they are placed. Asocial or grossly inappropriate behavior may be the patient's reaction to how he is treated, a manifestation of his conforming to the expectation that the surrounding society has for him. The so-called "deteriorated" state of many long-standing schizophrenic patients may be more of a reaction to hospitalization and social deprivation than the inevitable outcome of the disorder itself.

It is not yet clear to what extent the newer methods of treatment have altered long-term prognosis. It has become obvious that while drugs may shorten the hospitalization period for many schizophrenic patients, the interval between successive hospitalizations has also become shorter. In general, perhaps prognosis has not changed much over recent years; the experience of all therapies suggests that about one-third of the schizophrenic patients make adequate social adaptations; one-third make marginal social adaptations with occasional readmissions to hospitals and resumption of therapy; and one-third either deteriorate, commit suicide, or require long-term chronic hospitalization.

13 ∿∿∿∿∿∿∿∿∿∿∿∿∿∿∿∿∿∿∿∿∿∿∿∿∿∿

Psychotherapy

In the preceding discussion, it was suggested that psychotherapy often offers a feasible approach to the alleviation of the patient's psychological distress. This chapter will discuss the general rationale for psychotherapy—its definition, its application, and its underlying assumptions.

The term "psychotherapy" covers a multitude of activities executed by skilled, professional persons. Basic to all psychotherapy is the creation of a relationship between the patient and the therapist which is oriented toward the personal growth of the psychologically afflicted. Often, the goal of treatment may be symptom-removal; more frequently, the goal is to alter persisting patterns of behavior so that the individual will be able to adapt to future stresses without experiencing incapacitating symptoms, and in the light of new self-understanding.

The general assumption underlying psychotherapy is that personality disorders arise primarily out of interpersonal experiences, initially instigated in early childhood and currently perpetuated by the contemporary life situation. This assumption does not deny the role of genetic or organic factors in different disorders. In fact, organic factors may play varying roles in any disorder as it appears in different individuals. Nevertheless, the basic assumption underlying psychotherapy is that functional disorders are essentially the result of experiences with other people; that is, they are *learned reactions*. In terms of this assumption the psychotherapist attempts to resolve the underlying difficulty through a process of re-education of the patient in the context of a specific corrective experience with another person, the therapist.

In the process of psychotherapy, the therapist encourages the establishment of an emotional relationship between himself and the patient. In many ways, this relationship has as its prototype the child-parent relationship. In fact, in certain types of psychotherapy, it is said that treatment is not completed until the patient, in the context of his relationship with the therapist, has re-experienced and evolved new approaches toward the resolution of the major conflicts which were present in the child-parent relationship.

Whether or not such "re-living" of *all* major child-parent conflicts is necessary, it is inevitable that the patient transfers to the therapist the major conflicts and distortions which characterize his interactions with other people. Such *transference* constitutes the essence of the relationship with the therapist, and it is this transference which provides the therapist with the basic psychotherapeutic tools. The development of transference is facilitated by the patient's discomfort and his expectation of help from a knowledgeable authority. Most therapists try to maintain an atmosphere of neutrality so that the relationship which develops will mirror the patient's difficulties without being distorted by the therapist's own personality or provocations. For such reasons, emotional maturity and self-understanding are important attributes of the ideal therapist. In the context of a relationship with such a person, the patient may experience and re-experience his problems without the usual consequences which tend to perpetuate them.

Psychotherapeutic techniques vary greatly. Consequently, it is difficult to make generalizations which apply to all forms of psychotherapy. For example:

Some therapists believe that the major technique of psychotherapy is *interpretation,* i.e., pointing out to the patient the significance and meaning of his behavior. Other therapists feel that any interpretation comes best from the patient himself, and that verbalization of insight, when it occurs, is not the cause of improvement or cure, but rather the outcome of improvement.

Some therapists purposefully utilize techniques to foster the patient's dependency, at least in certain phases of the process. Other therapists would maintain that the patient must at all times be encouraged to be independent, self-reliant, and responsible for his own decisions.

Some therapists try to maintain a "blank screen" by being completely unrevealing of their own personal life and activities and by mirroring only what the patient himself presents. Other therapists believe that being a "real" person to the patient in an active interpersonal exchange is more beneficial.

Some therapists stress the distinction between thinking "with" the patient as opposed to thinking "about" him, trying solely to adopt the patient's frame of reference by understanding how he is thinking and feeling at the moment and then communicating that understanding to him.[1] Other therapists see the essential skill of the therapist to be that of being able to make proper interpretations about the patient's thoughts and feelings.

Some therapists believe that the experiences dealt with in psychotherapy should be primarily those in the present and that historical

---

[1] This emphasis particularly characterizes the so-called "nondirective" or "client-centered" school of psychotherapy, a group which has made an outstanding contribution to research on the process of psychotherapy. In terms of the supportive-interpretative distinction elaborated in later discussion above, this form of psychotherapy is difficult to categorize—although the technique appears more "supportive" than "interpretative," its goals often approximate those of interpretative psychotherapy. (See Rogers.)

antecedents of present behavior are relatively unimportant. Other therapists believe that the important goal of psychotherapy is to re-establish the link between past (early) experiences and present difficulties.

Some therapists believe that the experiences dealt with in psychotherapy should be *fantasied* experiences (dreams and free association). Other therapists believe that *reality* experiences are the more important data of psychotherapy.

In spite of the differences in technique represented by the many schools of psychotherapy, a large number of authorities think that the particular technique (or techniques) is probably not the most important aspect of psychotherapy since experimentally studied outcomes among the major schools do not appear to differ substantially. These authorities stress the elements common to all effective psychotherapies and believe that the therapeutic effort perhaps stems from these rather than from the specificities that may distinguish one approach from another.

COMMON ELEMENTS OF ALL EFFECTIVE PSYCHOTHERAPIES

Basic to any effective psychotherapy is a relationship of mutual respect, in which the patient senses the trustworthiness of the therapist and feels free to communicate without censoring or withholding. The structure of the ideal therapeutic relationship permits and encourages freedom of verbal self-expression without fear of censure or rejection. In the freedom and security of a relationship in which he feels he is understood, respected, and accepted, the patient is free to explore all areas of his life, moving progressively into those areas previously denied awareness, thereby coming both to experience and know himself more fully. Psychotherapy proceeds best when structured as a mutually collaborative effort; there is nothing magical about the transaction. For this reason, psychotherapy cannot proceed until there is a mutual agreement (at least implicit) that the patient has a problem which he desires to handle; that it is one which resides in him (rather than in his wife, or the boss, or reality); and that it is a problem amenable to psychotherapy with this particular therapist. Psychotherapy will probably have the greatest likelihood of success if the patient's suffering outweighs the rewards which accrue from having the disorder, that is, when the disadvantages clearly outweigh the advantages.

SUPPORTIVE VS. INTERPRETATIVE PSYCHOTHERAPY

It might be said that most psychotherapy includes some degree of both *support* and *interpretation*. Nevertheless, therapies sometimes have been characterized in terms of the extent to which they are primarily supportive or primarily interpretative.

SUPPORTIVE PSYCHOTHERAPY

This is indicated primarily in those instances when strengthening the patient's present defenses is all that can be safely undertaken *at that time,* or all that is practical, as with an elderly person. When there is a threat of a decompensation of present defenses, supportive psychotherapy may be required. In other instances, advanced age, present physical disabilities, or inflexibilities of the life situation may make a more ambitious undertaking impractical. The goal in these instances is usually to restore a prior (relatively) satisfactory adjustment, or to effect some adjustment within the existing personality structure of the patient. Therapy that is primarily supportive may later become more interpretative as the goals of treatment change.

A major principle of supportive therapy is to do nothing that will precipitate undue anxiety. For this reason, great care must be taken lest an important defense be jeopardized by the process of therapy. Emphasis is placed on the patient's current reality; free association, fantasy, and dream interpretation are usually not encouraged. Since inner controls may be weak, the therapist attempts to provide some degree of structure for the patient by the setting of realistic limits on the patient's behavior, giving advice and reassurance, and providing "support" when and where it is needed. Suggestion, persuasion, inspiration, direction, and exhortation may all be deliberately used by the therapist. Manipulation of the environment is sometimes utilized as a means of lessening stress on the patient. Because such therapy is often conducted with patients who are vulnerable to psychoses, the inherent dangers are great. Supportive therapy is extremely difficult to give since one must thoroughly understand the patient's defense structure to decide whether a maneuver will be supportive or not.

> A schizophrenic patient in a state of social recovery decompensated in the course of acting on the advice of his psychotherapist to take a vacation and to begin enjoying himself. While the advice of the therapist was seemingly "supportive," subsequent events confirmed the view that for this patient such advice was unwise. The patient relied on obsessive-compulsive defenses expressed in hard work to ward off extreme guilt, apparently related to the death of relatives in a concentration camp from which he had been able to maneuver his own release.

> Even such generally encouraging expressions as "I think you will get well" may be far from "supportive" for a patient whose defenses at present are weighted in favor of maintaining his illness. What may be supportive to the conscious wishes of the patient may be extremely threatening to his unconscious defenses and may lead him either to leave treatment or to become more seriously incapacitated.

During supportive therapy, it is important to be able to gauge the effectiveness of the patient's defense system—to know what is going on at all times. Symptoms may often serve important functions in maintaining a repair in defects of adjustment or in preventing further regression into a more serious illness. Hence, to remove a symptom precipitously may have disastrous consequences. Incidentally, some individuals incorrectly perceive supportive therapy as a cheaper, easier form of treatment, since its goals are often more modest ones, such as simply keeping the patient out of the hospital. Besides those situations in which it is all that can safely be undertaken, supportive therapy is also utilized when nothing more is deemed necessary. In a temporary grief reaction, reactive depression, situational reactions, adolescent turmoil, or in other transient crises occurring in a relatively intact personality, temporary support may be adequate to help the patient over a difficult period of adjustment.

INTERPRETATIVE PSYCHOTHERAPY

The goal of interpretative therapy, for the most part, is to change the basic personality structure of the patient rather than to achieve a more harmonious adjustment within or to it. For such a change to occur, the patient must have sufficient motivation to work for a long-range goal and to endure the accompanying frustration, anxiety, and sacrifice that adoption of such a goal entails. The patient's degree of personality integration must be adequate to tolerate anxiety precipitated by interpretation, the purpose of which is to put into carefully chosen, meaningful words the conflicts underlying the patient's difficulties with other people. For such an interpretation to be useful, it must be precise and concrete, and to be most effective it must be timed to coincide with the peak of emotional involvement for the patient.

The major forms of interpretative psychotherapy are *psychoanalysis* and *psychoanalytic psychotherapy*.

Psychoanalysis is based on the principles elucidated by Freud. The major techniques include free association and dream interpretation. A salient feature of psychoanalysis is the systematic investigation and interpretation of the transference relationship which develops between the patient and his analyst, as well as an analysis of the patient's emotional resistances which have led to the distortions in his relationships with others. The goal of psychoanalysis is the achievement by the patient of insight into his unconscious conflicts along with an extensive alteration of personality structure, which both together are manifest by changes in formerly maladaptive behavior. In its classical form, psychoanalysis is an intense (frequently five hours a week), long-term process. Briefer methods and modifications of the technique by many so-called "neo-Freudians" [1] have given rise to many different schools of psychoanalysis. Never-

---

[1] This group would include Horney, Sullivan, Reik, Adler, Rado.

theless, some authorities prefer to maintain the term "psycho-analysis" for psychotherapy in the classical sense alone, as originated by Freud and his direct followers.

In contrast to classical psychoanalysis as just described, *psychoanalytic psychotherapy* utilizes the insights of Freud and his followers, but with a greater degree of flexibility of approach. Goals of treatment may be circumscribed and related to specific problem areas. Since less emphasis may be given to a systematic investigation and interpretation of the transference relationship, less emphasis may also be placed on the therapist's maintaining a "blank screen." He may, in fact, actively relate to and with the patient, in a more typically natural way than that which characterizes classical psychoanalysis. Rather than free association and dream productions, detailed reporting of ongoing interpersonal relationships, directed by relevant questioning by the therapist, may constitute the primary approach. Supportive and re-educative techniques may be used with greater freedom than in classical psychoanalysis.

Modification of techniques has extended the usefulness of psychotherapy to such groups as schizophrenic patients and "borderline" cases which would not be amenable to classical psychoanalysis. With schizophrenic patients, for example, the usual type of interpretation is frequently found useless since often these patients are quite aware of the symbolic significance of their communications. Since these patients often have difficulty distinguishing between fantasy and reality, free association (unrestrained fantasy) is seldom utilized. It has been found to be most helpful to work with reality problems with these patients. Therapy in these circumstances is conducted on a face-to-face relationship (rather than with the patient on a couch), and with great flexibility regarding not only the frequency but also the length of sessions.

* * *

Psychotherapy of any type is often a long-term process, since early and long-established patterns of behavior are resistant to change. Although relief of symptoms sometimes can be easily accomplished in a brief period of time, enduring personality change usually can occur only after new learnings have been tried, modified, and tried again, in the context of a relationship characterized by nonpossessive caring for the patient by the therapist.

Undoubtedly the future will give evidence of great advances in the scientific understanding of interpersonal relationships which occur in psychotherapy. Long considered an art, psychotherapy in recent years has become the focus of intensive research efforts in the behavioral sciences. The past decade has witnessed increasing advances in the formulation of specific, rational therapies suitable for specific symptom complexes. As a science, psychotherapy is in its early stages. Nevertheless, judiciously applied, it offers a highly effective means of increasing the happiness, productivity, and well-being of the patient.

Appendix A

Glossary

ABREACTION: a release of feelings or emotions through reliving (in fantasy or action) a situation previously denied to conscious awareness.

AFFECT: subjective feeling state or emotion, e.g., depression, guilt, anger, anxiety.

AFFECTIVE DISORDER: an illness in which moods or emotions are predominant; in psychotic form, includes psychotic depressive reactions and manic-depressive psychoses.

AMBIVALENCE: coexistence of opposing feelings, usually involving both love and hate.

ANAL STAGE: stage of personality development occurring roughly between one-and-a-half and three years at which time the problem of habit training, involving control, particularly in relation to bowel training, becomes prominent. The resolution of conflicts characteristic of this period may give rise to enduring personality traits subsumed under "anal" traits—obstinacy, stinginess, and orderliness.

ANAMNESIS: patient's recall of his developmental history prior to onset of his illness.

ANXIETY: an affect characterized by feelings of apprehension, uncertainty, and helplessness which are not attached to a real, external danger.

AUTISM: a form of thinking, largely subjective, idiosyncratic, and without sufficient regard for reality; characteristic of schizophrenia.

AUTOEROTISM: sexual self-gratification, masturbation.

CASTRATION ANXIETY: apprehension of bodily harm or loss of manhood or masculinity, derived from apprehension of threat to the genitals or injury to the body; first arises at the oedipal stage of development (age, three to six years).

139

CATATONIA: a form of schizophrenia in which motor symptoms predominate.

CATHARSIS: a release of tension and anxiety through abreaction.

CATHEXIS: investment of emotional feeling and significance in an object or idea.

CHARACTER DISORDER: a disorder distinguished by difficulties in conforming to cultural and social moral expectations with relatively little personal discomfort, showing few or none of the major symptoms of a neurosis or a psychosis.

COMPULSION: a recurrent action or ritual which is repeated in a perseverative way as a means of avoiding extreme anxiety.

CONFABULATION: filling in of a memory loss by relating of experiences without regard for truth.

CONFLICT: a distinct clash between two or more impulses or desires within the personality.

CONVERSION: process by which an emotional conflict is unconsciously transformed into a physical manifestation, often with symbolic meaning.

COUNTERTRANSFERENCE: irrational attitudes, feelings, and fantasies experienced by the therapist in relation to a patient (see *Transference*).

DECOMPENSATION: the failure or breakdown of existing defenses leading to more pathological behavior.

DEFENSE (mechanism): unconscious mental process employed to resolve conflicts or anxiety, e.g., projection, repression, denial, reaction formation, undoing.

DELUSION: a firm and fixed idea or set of ideas which are not consistent with reality and which are not influenced by logic, common sense, or rational explanation.

DEMENTIA PRAECOX: obsolete descriptive term for schizophrenia, formerly based on a conception of the disorder as being characterized by an early onset and involving ultimate deterioration (dementia).

DENIAL: an unconscious process which involves the avoidance of a painful or anxiety-producing reality by refusing to admit its existence.

DEPERSONALIZATION: feelings of unreality concerning the self or the outside world.

DEPRESSION: (1) an affect involving a feeling of sadness, dejection, loneliness, and loss of interest; (2) a clinical syndrome characterized by a depressive affect, multiple somatic manifestations, and loss of self-esteem.

DETERIORATION: mental impairment, traditionally assumed to be irreversible and progressive. As it occurs in schizophrenia, impairment is not necessarily irreversible or progressive. Terms "deficit" or "impairment" avoid the unwarranted implications suggested by the term "deterioration."

DISPLACEMENT: the process by which a feeling or emotion is unconsciously transferred from its object to a more acceptable substitute.

DISSOCIATION: the separation or splitting off of a segment of the personality in such a way that conscious awareness or control of the segment is lost.

DON JUANISM: a compulsive, exaggerated need to seduce women, often motivated by denied and unconscious homosexual impulses.

ECHOLALIA: repetition of words or groups of words echoing something said by another person; frequently found in catatonic schizophrenia.

EGO BOUNDARY: hypothetical line separating the self from objects in the environment, a differentiation basic to reality testing.

ELECTROCONVULSIVE THERAPY (electroshock, ECT, or EST): method of treatment usually given three to five times a week, involving application of electrical current bitemporally, usually to produce unconsciousness and a seizure state. Treatment has been useful in relieving depressions; method has been somewhat displaced by use of pharmacotherapy.

EMOTION: subjective feeling state, e.g., love, hate, fear, anxiety, grief.

EMPATHY: ability to sense the feelings and behavior of another person.

EUPHORIA: exaggerated feeling of well-being which is not realistically based.

FETISHISM: a disorder in which sexual excitement and gratification are produced by an object invested with abnormal sexual significance, such as a shoe, garment, hair.

FIXATION: an arrest in development, generally of psychological origin. The term *fixation* (arrest) is usually differentiated from *regression,* referring to a return to an earlier stage of development.

FREE ASSOCIATION: the act of relinquishing conscious control over one's thoughts and speaking freely of whatever comes into one's mind.

FRUSTRATION: the blocking of goal-directed activity; a frequently stated hypothesis is that *frustration* leads to *aggression.*

FUNCTIONAL ILLNESS: illness of emotional origin without known structural or organic causes.

GRANDIOSITY: unrealistic ideas of self-importance.

GRIEF: normal response to a loss of a loved person or object, characterized by sadness and dejection.

HALLUCINATION: a false sensory perception of an object not actually present, hence, an *abnormal* phenomenon, as opposed to misinterpretations of stimuli which are present (illusions).

HOMOSEXUAL PANIC: an acute, severe attack of anxiety based on unconscious conflicts about homosexuality. Although these episodes are usually of relatively brief duration, the extent of the disorganization generally warrants a diagnosis of *schizophrenia*.

HYPOCHONDRIASIS: an internalization of body-image problems represented by a persistent overconcern with the health of the body.

HYSTERIA: a neurotic disorder in which anxiety is converted into physical symptoms via the mechanism of conversion.

IDENTIFICATION: the process of becoming like something or someone, based on an internalization of the image of the external object.

ILLUSION: a false perception in any of the five senses, based on a misinterpretation of a stimulus actually present (see *Hallucination*).

IMPULSE: a striving, motive, or need, gratification of which leads to satisfaction.

INCORPORATION: the process of taking something into oneself; in the literal sense, via the mouth.

INSIGHT: self-understanding.

INSULIN THERAPY: method of treatment designed by Manfred Sakel, increasingly replaced by pharmacotherapy for treatment of schizophrenia. Technique usually involves daily administration of insulin achieving a coma-producing hypoglycemia.

INTELLIGENCE QUOTIENT (IQ): an index of mental brightness, expressing the relationship between mental age and chronological age.

INTROJECTION: sometimes used synonymously with the term *identification;* introjection represents a less adaptive and more primitive way of adjusting than is characterized by the process of identification.

INVOLUTIONAL PSYCHOSIS: a psychotic disorder, frequently characterized by depression or paranoid ideas, occurring at the time of the climacteric.

ISOLATION (ISOLATION OF AFFECT): an unconscious process by which experiences, impressions, and memories are separated from their emotional significance and are experienced without feeling or affect.

LA BELLE INDIFFÉRENCE: inappropriate lack of concern about one's disability, frequently found in hysterical disorders in which the disability is serving symbolic gratifications.

MANIA: an abnormal state characterized by flight of ideas, overactivity, and elation.

MANIC-DEPRESSIVE PSYCHOSIS: a psychotic disorder, typically recurrent and cyclical, involving alterations of mood.

MELANCHOLIA: pathological state of sadness and depression.

NEUROSIS: a psychological disorder in which reality testing remains relatively intact but in which unconscious conflicts give rise to such symptoms as anxiety, feelings of depression, unreasonable fears, doubts, obsessions, and psychogenically determined physical ills.

OBSESSION: a recurring thought or idea which enters into consciousness without voluntary control.

OEDIPAL: term which refers to the repressed desire to replace the parent of the same sex in the love of the parent of the opposite sex; *oedipal stage* refers to that period of development (approximately age two-and-a-half to six) when unconscious rivalry with the parent of the opposite sex becomes most prominent.

ORAL STAGE: a stage of personality development, particularly the first year of life, when oral dependency predominates in the relationship between the child and his environment.

PANIC: overpowering anxiety and fear leading to disorganized behavior.

PARANOIA: disorder in which delusions of grandeur and/or of persecution predominate.

PHOBIA: a persistent fear attached to an object or situation which is objectively not a source of danger and serves symbolically to represent the real source of danger.

PROJECTION: the unconscious mental process by which emotionally unacceptable impulses are rejected and attributed to (projected onto) others.

PROJECTIVE TECHNIQUES: methods of personality assessment utilizing ambiguous or relatively unstructured stimuli to elicit the subject's interpretation; e.g., Rorschach Test, Thematic Apperception Test.

PSYCHIATRY: a medical specialty which deals with mental illness and personality disorders.

PSYCHIATRIST: a physician whose medical specialty is the practice of psychiatry.

PSYCHOANALYSIS: (1) a theory of personality development, originally developed by Freud, modified by followers; (2) a method of therapy developed by Freud in which free association and dream interpretation are major techniques.

PSYCHOANALYST: one who practices psychotherapy by the technique of psychoanalysis, most often having a medical degree although other specialists are also trained in this technique.

PSYCHODYNAMICS: the science of human behavior which attempts to explain and predict human behavior in terms of motivations and drives which are largely emotional and unconscious in character.

PSYCHOLOGIST: a specialist in the science of human behavior, ordinarily requiring a Ph.D.

PSYCHONEUROSIS: term used synonymously with neurosis.

PSYCHOPATH: a person whose behavior is predominantly antisocial or amoral, but who experiences minimal guilt or anxiety. This term is in somewhat ill-repute as a designation for a specific diagnostic group; more frequently used as an adjective (*psychopathic*) to characterize antisocial behavior which may actually appear in the context of any diagnostic disorder.

PSYCHOPATHOLOGIST: a specialist in psychopathology; the term generally includes psychiatrists, psychologists, and psychoanalysts.

PSYCHOSIS: a severe disturbance in psychological functioning in which the individual's ability to distinguish, evaluate, and test reality is defective.

PSYCHOSOMATIC ILLNESS: physical disorders in which psychogenic factors are of predominant etiological importance in the initiation and perpetuation of the pathophysiological process.

PSYCHOTHERAPY: treatment through psychological means, basic to which is the interpersonal relationship of patient and therapist.

RATIONALIZATION: the process in which one gives socially acceptable reasons for his behavior rather than the real (often unconscious) reasons.

REACTION FORMATION: a process in which behavior and attitudes are adopted which are the direct opposite of impulses which the individual cannot directly express; e.g., a substitution of love for hate.

REGRESSION: a return to a less mature level of behavior as a result of frustration (see *Fixation*).

REPRESSION: the process of exclusion from awareness (or consciousness) of those impulses, feelings, memories, or experiences which otherwise would precipitate anxiety. Repressed material continues to seek expression through derivatives which often become manifest in the form of symptoms.

RESISTANCE: a manifestation of a defense against bringing repressed thoughts into awareness; frequently experienced in the process of psychotherapy.

SCHIZOPHRENIA: a severe psychosis in which the major disturbance is reflected in a disorder of thinking and the thought processes.

Catatonic: a type of schizophrenia in which motor symptoms are prominent, either of stupor or overactivity.

Hebephrenic: a type of schizophrenia characterized by extreme silliness and inappropriateness of behavior.

Latent: a form of schizophrenia not directly manifested in behavior but indicating a potentiality for decompensation into an overt schizophrenic state.

Paranoid: a type of schizophrenia in which delusions of grandeur and/or of persecution predominate.

Process versus reactive: a distinction sometimes made between forms of schizophrenia which occur without apparent external precipitating causes, usually with slow, insidious onset and of poor prognosis (process), and those forms which appear as a response to a specific environmental stress, usually of more sudden onset and better prognosis (reactive). Although this distinction cuts across the traditional classifications of schizophrenia, the process type would come closest to the *simple* and *hebephrenic* types; the reactive type would come closest to *catatonic* and *paranoid* types.

Pseudoneurotic: a form of schizophrenia in which the psychotic process is masked by numerous seemingly neurotic symptoms, pervasive anxiety, and a chaotic sexuality.

Schizo-affective: a form of schizophrenia in which manic-depressive features coexist with typically schizophrenic ones.

Simple: a type of schizophrenia characterized by apathy, indifference, withdrawal, and lack of ambition.

SECONDARY GAIN: indirect advantage received from an illness (e.g., attention, sympathy, care) as opposed to its primary effects.

SENILE PSYCHOSIS: severe mental disorder based on impairment of brain tissue occurring in old age.

SHOCK TREATMENT: physical methods of therapy including electroconvulsive therapy (ECT) and insulin coma treatment.

SOCIOPATHIC: Behavior which is out of conformity with society and the prevailing culture, frequently antisocial or amoral; sometimes used synonomously with *psychopathic.*

SUPEREGO: that part of the personality developed through the internalization of family, social, and cultural norms; broadly defined, it may include two aspects: conscience and ego ideal.

SUPPRESSION: the conscious inhibition of a thought or impulse, usually differentiated from *repression* which is an unconscious process.

TRANSFERENCE: attitudes, feelings, and fantasies which a patient has about his therapist which are irrational in the sense that they are based on attitudes formerly associated with a parent or other significant person.

UNCONSCIOUS: portion of mental functioning not available to recall.

UNDOING: the process in which something already done is symbolically canceled out (undone) as if it has never occurred; frequently the mechanism underlying a *compulsion.*

APPENDIX B

Outline for Psychiatric History and Mental Status Examination

The purpose of an outline for a *psychiatric history* is to provide a useful recording in succinct and precise terms of the patient's illness in context of the patient's life situation, supplemented by specific information of a biographical nature concerning the patient's life during the stages of developmental maturation, together with the family history pertinent to the personal history of the patient. A *mental status examination* is a formalized routine for evaluation of behavior, emotion, and mental state, utilizing specific standardized questions.

An adequate history and mental state examination should allow the interviewer tentatively to formulate aspects of classification, psychodynamics, and psychogenesis which will lead to diagnosis, prognosis, and a plan for management. A suggested form for these is as follows:

Identifying data

Name of patient:
Address:
Sex:
Age:
Marital state:
Occupation:
Race:
Reason for referral:
Name of referral source:
Date of examination:

Chief complaints

(Verbatim listing of the patient's complaints to the interviewer, including duration.)

History of present illness

(A narrative description in chronological order of the development of the problems for which the patient seeks help at this time, including precipitating events. The facts, situations, and circumstances relative to the occurrence of the first symptoms should be elucidated in detail. In this section, describe the patient's behavior, actions, physical symptoms, psychological attitudes, emotional symptoms and responses.)

Development history (personal history)

(A brief and precise historical account of the patient as a person during various phases of life, beginning with the facts and place of birth):

Childhood: Define the experiences of childhood, including habit-training experiences, specifically eating, bowel habit, sleeping, and playing, with particular references to childhood illnesses, injuries, or operations; attitudes concerning starting to school; school experiences; social and friendship patterns; adjustment at school; academic success and failures; truancy patterns; asocial behavior; physical development (body defects, congenital defects, physical makeup); early sexual experiences and development; nightmares and recurrent childhood dreams; childhood psychopathy (enuresis, temper tantrums, tics, etc.)

Adolescence: Age of onset of puberty, menstrual history, adolescent friendship patterns, scholastic accomplishments and adaptation, dating patterns, body concerns, sexual experiences, nervous habits, conflict with the law.

Adult life: Educational and intellectual attainments, occupational adjustment, sexual adjustment, courtship patterns, attitudes surrounding sex, money habits, pleasure capacity, major concerns and preoccupations, social adjustment, military experience, religious attitudes, hobbies, ambitions and life goals, predominant personality characteristics, and attitude toward the self.

Family history

(Pertinent family history should be summarized, including a description of the significant figures in the patient's previous and present life (mother, father, siblings, spouse, children). Describe significant areas of family conflict, as well as the positive relationships. Where possible, indicate not only the reality aspects of the home and family life, but also the patient's thoughts and feelings about them. Indicate history of physical or psychological disturbances in the family, including significant family history of migraine, epilepsy, alcoholism, mental illnesses, with special reference to genetically transmissible illnesses. Responses to deaths and other critical events in the family should also be indicated.)

Previous physical and emotional illnesses and treatment

(Type; duration; treatment; response to treatment; relationship to present illness.)

Mental status

1. General appearance, attitude, and behavior.
(Manner of dress; gait; posture; facial expression; general impression on the interviewer; general statement on degree of cooperativeness: accessibility, alertness, tenseness, restlessness, friendliness, tidiness, disorderedness, broodiness, agitation, negativism, indifference, stuporous, stereotypic behavior.)

2. General motility.
(Physical characteristics; motor activity: normal, compulsive, bizarre, retarded; pressure of activity; handwringing; pacing; crying.)

3. Speech and thinking.
(Disorders of speech: scanning, hesitant, slurred, nasal, stuttering, aphasia, etc.
Disorders of thinking:
   Production: flow of thought, acceleration of thought, retardation of thought.
   Continuity: clear, coherent, relevant, rambling, circumstantial, perseverative, flight of ideas, blocked.
   Content: formation of concepts; handling of ideas; anxieties; fears; obsessions; phobias; hypochondriacal preoccupations; body-image concerns; autism; ideas of reference; ideas of influence; self-depreciation; suicidal ideas; somatic delusions; systematized delusions; self-referential ideas; hallucinations.)

4. Emotional state.
(Interviewer should evaluate the appropriateness of emotional responses during the interview as well as the degree of emotional responsivity with specific reference to loss of emotional contact. Indicate disturbances in regulation of emotions; mood swings; control of emotions; anxieties; feelings of unreality; perplexity; agitation; irritability; depression; apathy; elation.)

5. Somatic functioning.
(Range of physical symptoms; sleep disturbances; eating, appetite, and weight disturbances; bowel regularity; sexual disturbances.)

6. Mental grasp.

Orientation:

  Time:

  Place:

  Identity:

Memory:

  Remote (birth date, age, grade in school, etc.)

  Recent (food of last meal, present date, etc.)

Retention:

  Digit span:

    Forward:

    Reversed:

  Calculation:

    Serial 7's subtraction:

    Simple addition or multiplication:

  General information:

    Recall of Presidents:

    Significant events:

    Current news:

Judgment:

(General appreciation of social convention; e.g., difference between a lie and a mistake, etc.)

Estimated intellectual level and present efficiency:

Insight:

Attitude of patient toward his symptoms:

Plan for the future:

  7. Formulation.

a. Summary of patient's problems in the light of his behavior, character traits, and psychological disturbances, with affective and somatic disturbances:

b. Outstanding features of the genetic, familial, and life situational influences as revealed from all examinations:

c. Explanation of symptoms and origin of the patient's problems in terms of the developmental history:

d. Diagnostic impression:

e. Plan for management:

(Realistic plan, indicating kind of treatment, ancillary therapies, need for hospitalization, or for commitment or guardianship. Potential transference problems should be indicated; estimate of prognosis.)

Appendix C

Psychological Testing

Psychological tests, when properly interpreted by an experienced psychologist, often help clarify important aspects of classification, psychodynamics, and psychogenesis.

Typical referral problems which may constitute the basis for referring a patient to a psychologist include the following:

1. *Level of intellectual functioning.*

By means of well-standardized intelligence tests, it is possible to determine the patient's general level of intellectual functioning. The most meaningful report will include not only the Intellectual Quotient (IQ), but will also indicate relative intellectual strengths and weaknesses in terms of such abilities as general range of information, memory, arithmetic ability, abstracting ability, social judgment, etc. If the patient is not operating at his typical level of achievement, it may be possible to infer what his potential would be. The patterning of abilities may relate to such varied decisions as school placement, commitment to an institution for mental defectives, job placement, or potentialities for psychotherapy.

2. *Organic impairment.*

Psychological tests are often useful in determining whether the patient's particular strengths and weaknesses are indicative of brain damage. Characteristic psychomotor disturbances may be reflected in the patient's graphomotor productions, such as the Bender-Gestalt test. Organically based memory difficulties may be revealed through tests which differentiate recent learning from early or remote learning. Typical disabilities (e.g., the patient's becoming perplexed, confused, being unable to improve his performance with practice and tending to perseverate on a certain response) are often highlighted in the projective techniques, since the test stimuli are ambiguous (unstructured) and offer no clues for appropriate responses.

3. *Differential diagnosis.*

Psychological tests may clarify important aspects of classification and diagnosis. The distinction between neurotic and psychotic disorders is often particularly relevant, a distinction based on the patient's ability to evaluate reality. An inherent advantage of many psychological tests is the availability of normative data for the major diagnostic groups with which the patient's performance may be compared and evaluated. The projective techniques are particularly useful since, although presumably having no "right" or "wrong" answers, they nevertheless establish the conventionality of the patient's perceptions and the logic of his thought processes. If the patient's ability to evaluate reality is intact in even the highly unstructured situations represented by the projective techniques, the possibility of a psychosis is unlikely.

4. *Personality evaluation.*

Psychological tests may help clarify the major motivational forces operating within a patient, those of which he is both aware and unaware. They will reveal his characteristic thought processes, his major interests and preoccupations, his characteristic defenses utilized to allay anxiety, and his vulnerability to greater personality disorganization. These findings often have relevance to such specific questions as possible suicidal risk, likelihood of assaultive acting out, prognosis, need for hospitalization.

5. *Potentialities for therapy.*

Psychological tests may reveal strengths and weaknesses which have implications for the choice of a particular kind of treatment. Limitations in intellectual ability, inability to identify or to form an effective relationship with a psychotherapist, intensity of the depressive affect, stability of present defenses, and the inferred psychogenesis of the disorder are examples of factors which may lead to the choice of a given kind of therapy: drugs, electroshock, supportive psychotherapy, interpretative psychotherapy, manipulation of the environment, etc.

6. *Evaluation of change.*

Psychological tests may be used to evaluate a change occurring over a period of time. For example, improvement in psychotherapy may be corroborated by changes occurring in test results; effects of brain surgery may be objectively verified by means of testing conducted at appropriate intervals prior to and after surgery. For purposes of reevaluation, some tests have alternate forms which are comparable; in other instances, the same test can be used if appropriate consideration is given to possible practice effects.

Some important psychological tests

INTELLIGENCE TESTS *Stanford-Binet Scales.* Developed out of efforts formalized by Alfred Binet, a French psychologist, in the first decade of
this century. Its aim is to measure general intelligence. Individually
administered, it expresses test scores in terms of age levels of performance. To the two alternative scales (forms L and M of the 1937 revision)
has been added a 1960 revision called L-M which is a combination of
subtests from the L and M scales. All scales cover the range from two
years to the highly superior adult level. Index of developmental level
is the mental age. Index of brightness is the IQ (mental age divided by
the chronological age multiplied by 100). For subjects of 16 and over,
the chronological age divisor for computing an IQ is 15.

Wechsler Adult Intelligence Scale (WAIS). A revision of the Wechsler-
Bellevue Intelligence Scales. This is probably the most popular individual intelligence test in clinical practice. Standardized for various age
groups from 16–64 years, it is not dependent on the concept of "mental
age." It is individually administered and consists of eleven subtests. Six
tests are verbal in nature; five tests are performance. Yields both a
verbal IQ and a performance IQ, as well as a full-scale IQ. Scores on
subtests are assumed to have diagnostic significance. A form for children
is also available, Wechsler Intelligence Scale for Children (WISC).

TESTS OF PERSONALITY *Minnesota Multiphasic Personality Inventory*
(MMPI). Consists of 550 questions which the subject sorts into one of
three categories, "True," "False," or "Cannot say." Nine clinical scales
have been developed: hypochondriasis, depression, hysteria, psychopathic
deviate, masculinity-femininity, paranoia, psychasthenia, schizophrenia,
mania; also four validating scales to determine test-taking attitude,
defensiveness, etc. Scales were empirically validated in terms of what
various diagnostic groups actually report about themselves.

Rorschach Test. Devised by Hermann Rorschach, a Swiss psychiatrist.
The most widely used projective technique, it consists of ten symmetrical,
ambiguous inkblots, five in varying shades of gray to black and five
in other colors. Test instructions essentially are, "What might this be?"
Each response is systemmatically scored for area of blot used, characteristic of blot determining the response, accuracy of form perception,
content, conventionality of response, etc.

Thematic Apperception Test (TAT). Devised by Henry Murray and
Christiana Morgan. Variation for children (Bellak Children's Apperception Test) and for adolescents (Symonds Picture Story Test). The
TAT consists of nineteen pictures and one blank card. Subject is asked
to make up a story about each picture, including what is happening

now, what led up to this scene, and what the outcome will be. Pictures vary in their degree of ambiguity; only selected pictures need be used. Stories reveal dominant drives, emotions, sentiments, complexes, and conflicts of the story teller.

Draw-a-Person Test. Drawing of a person is assumed to represent an expression of the self or the body in the environment. Interpretative principles rest largely on Schilder's concept of "body-image." Originally used as a measure of intelligence; now classified as a protective technique. Variations of test include "Draw a house, tree, and person" (HTP) and "Draw an animal."

Bender-Gestalt Test. Perceptual motor test in which nine simple geometric figures are copied by the subject, followed by a test of recall, in which the subject is asked to draw from memory as many as he can. Although conceived by Lauretta Bender as a test of maturation, it is increasingly used as a projective technique with interpretation made in terms of spatial organization of designs, line quality, alterations, distortions, rotations, assumed symbolic meaning of individual designs, etc.

Sentence Completion Test. A wide range of sentence completion tests is available which presents series of sentence stems which are to be completed by the subject to make sentences; e.g., "I often wished . . ."; "My mother . . ."; "I sometimes feel that . . ." This generally reveals conscious attitudes, feelings, wishes, anxieties, and so forth.

Appendix D

Bibliography

General

Arieti, S. (ed.). *American Handbook of Psychiatry*, Vols. I–II. New York: Basic Books, 1959.

Cameron, N. *Personality Development and Psychopathology*. Boston: Houghton Mifflin Company, 1963.

Cammer, L. *Outline of Psychiatry*. New York: McGraw-Hill Company, Inc., 1962.

Engel, G. L. *Psychological Development in Health and Disease*. Philadelphia: W. B. Saunders Company, 1962.

English, O. S., and Pearson, G. H. *Emotional Problems of Living: Avoiding the Neurotic Pattern*. Rev. ed. New York: W. W. Norton & Company, Inc., 1955.

Erikson, E. H. *Childhood and Society*. New York: W. W. Norton & Company, Inc., 1950.

Fenichel, O. *The Psychoanalytic Theory of Neurosis*. New York: W. W. Norton & Company, Inc., 1945.

Freud, S. *The Standard Edition of the Complete Psychological Works of Sigmund Freud*. London: Hogarth, 1953.

Henderson, D., and Batchelor, I. R. C. *Henderson and Gillespie's Textbook of Psychiatry for Students and Practitioners*. 9th ed. New York: Oxford University Press, 1962.

Hunt, J., McV. (ed.). *Personality and the Behavior Disorders*. Vols. I–II. New York: Ronald Press Co., 1944.

Nemiah, J. C. *Foundations of Psychopathology*. New York: Oxford University Press, 1961.

Noyes, A. P., and Kolb, L. C. *Modern Clinical Psychiatry*. 6th ed. Philadelphia: W. B. Saunders Company, 1963.

Chapter 1

Bowlby, J. *Maternal Care and Mental Health*. Geneva: World Health Organization, 1951.

Deutsch, Helene. *Psychoanalysis of the Neurosis*. London: Hogarth, 1932.

French, T. *Integration of Behavior*. Vol. I. Chicago: University of Chicago Press, 1952.

Freud, A. *The Ego and the Mechanisms of Defence*. London: Hogarth, 1937.

Freud, S. "Three Essays on the Theory of Sexuality." *The Standard Edition of the Complete Psychological Works of Sigmund Freud*. Vol. VII. London: Hogarth, 1953.

Hartmann, H., and Kris, E. "The Genetic Approach in Psychoanalysis." *The Psychoanalytic Study of the Child*. Vol. I. New York: International Universities Press, 1945.

Money, J. "An Examination of the Concept of Psychodynamics." *Psychiatry*. 17:325, 1954.

Ribble, M. "Infantile Experience in Relation to Personality Development." *Personality and the Behavior Disorders*. Vol. II (J. McV. Hunt, ed.). New York: Ronald Press Co., 1944.

Chapter 2

Arieti, S. "Manic-Depressive Psychosis." *American Handbook of Psychiatry*. Vol. I (S. Arieti, ed.). New York: Basic Books, 1959.

Bellak, L., et al. *Manic-Depressive Psychosis and Allied Conditions*. New York: Grune & Stratton, Inc., 1952.

Cohen, M. B., et al. "An Intensive Study of Twelve Cases of Manic-Depressive Psychosis." *Psychiatry*. 17:103, 1954.

Freud, S. "Mourning and Melancholia." *The Standard Edition of the Complete Psychological Works of Sigmund Freud*. Vol. XIV. London: Hogarth, 1957.

Greenacre, Phyllis (ed.). *Affective Disorders: Psychoanalytic Contributions to Their Study*. New York: International Universities Press, 1953.

Hoch, P. H., and Zubin, J. (eds.). *Depression*. New York: Grune & Stratton, Inc., 1954.

Kallmann, F. J. *Heredity in Health and Mental Disorder*. New York: W. W. Norton & Company, Inc., 1953.

Lewin, B. *The Psychoanalysis of Elation*. New York: W. W. Norton & Company, Inc., 1950.

Lindemann, E. "Symptomatology and Management of Acute Grief." *Amer. J. Psychiat.* 101:141, 1944.

Nemiah, J. C. "The Psychopathology of Depression." *Foundations of Psychopathology.* New York: Oxford University Press, 1961.

Rado, S. "Psychodynamics of Depression from the Etiologic Point of View." *Psychosom. Med.* 13:51, 1951.

Chapter 3

Freud, A. *The Ego and the Mechanisms of Defence.* London: Hogarth, 1937.

Freud, S. *The Problem of Anxiety.* New York: W. W. Norton & Company, Inc., 1936.

Funkenstein, D. H.; King, S. H.; and Drolette, M. E. *The Mastery of Stress.* Cambridge: Harvard University Press, 1957.

Hoch, P. H. "Biosocial Aspects of Anxiety." *Anxiety.* Hoch, P. H., and Zubin, J. (eds.). New York: Grune & Stratton, Inc., 1950.

Horney, K. *Neurosis and Human Growth.* New York: W. W. Norton & Company, Inc., 1950.

May, R. *The Meaning of Anxiety.* New York: Ronald Press Co., 1950.

Selye, H. *The Stress of Life.* New York: McGraw-Hill Company, Inc., 1956.

Sullivan, H. S. *The Interpersonal Theory of Psychiatry.* New York: W. W. Norton & Company, Inc., 1953.

Chapter 4

Fenichel, O. *The Psychoanalytic Theory of Neurosis.* New York: W. W. Norton & Company, Inc., 1945.

Freud, A. *The Ego and the Mechanisms of Defence.* London: Hogarth, 1937.

Freud, S. "Analysis of a Phobia in a Five-Year-Old Boy." *The Standard Edition of the Complete Psychological Works of Sigmund Freud.* Vol. X. London: Hogarth, 1955.

Friedman, P. "The Phobias." *American Handbook of Psychiatry.* Vol. I (S. Arieti, ed.). New York: Basic Books, 1959.

Lewin, B. D. "Phobic Symptoms and Dream Interpretation." *Psychoanal. Quart.* 21:295, 1952.

Chapter 5

Abse, D. W. "Hysteria." *American Handbook of Psychiatry.* Vol. I (S. Arieti, ed.). New York: Basic Books, 1959.

Alexander, F. *Psychosomatic Medicine.* New York: W. W. Norton & Company, Inc., 1950.

Bender, M. B. *Disorders in Perception.* Springfield, Ill.: Charles C. Thomas, Publisher, 1952.

Binger, C. *The Doctor's Job.* New York: W. W. Norton & Company, Inc., 1945.

Chodoff, P. "The Re-examination of Some Aspects of Conversion Hysteria." *Psychiatry.* 17:75, 1954.

Chrzanowski, G. "Neurasthenia and Hypochondriasis." *American Handbook of Psychiatry.* Vol. I (S. Arieti, ed.). New York: Basic Books, 1959.

Dunbar, F. *Mind and Body: Psychosomatic Medicine.* New York: Random House, Inc., 1955.

Engel, G. *Psychological Development in Health and Disease.* Philadelphia: W. B. Saunders Company, 1962.

Freud, S. "Fragment of an Analysis of a Case of Hysteria." *The Standard Edition of the Complete Psychological Works of Sigmund Freud.* Vol. VII. London: Hogarth, 1953.

Kolb, L. C. *The Painful Phantom: Psychology, Physiology and Treatment.* Springfield, Ill.: Charles C. Thomas, Publisher, 1954.

——— "Disturbances of the Body-Image." *American Handbook of Psychiatry.* Vol. I (S. Arieti, ed.). New York: Basic Books, 1959.

Lidz, T. "General Concepts of Psychosomatic Medicine." *American Handbook of Psychiatry.* Vol. I (S. Arieti, ed.). New York: Basic Books, 1959.

Schilder, P. *The Image and Appearance of the Human Body.* New York: International Universities Press, 1950.

Szasz, T. S. "A Contribution to the Psychology of Bodily Feelings." *Psychoanal. Quart.* 26:25, 1957.

Chapter 6

Angyal, A. "Evasion of Growth." *Am. J. Psychiat.* 110:358, 1953.

English, O. S., and Pearson, G. H. S. *Common Neuroses of Children and Adults.* New York: W. W. Norton & Company, Inc., 1937.

Fenichel, O. *The Psychoanalytic Theory of Neurosis.* New York: W. W. Norton & Company, Inc., 1945.

Rado, S. "Obsessive Behavior." *American Handbook of Psychiatry.* Vol. I (S. Arieti, ed.). New York: Basic Books, 1959.

Weissman, P. "Ego and Superego in Obsessional Character and Neurosis." *Psychoanal. Quart.* 23:529, 1954.

Chapter 7

Benedek, T. F. "Sexual Functions in Women and Their Disturbance." *American Handbook of Psychiatry.* Vol. I (S. Arieti, ed.). New York: Basic Books, 1959.

Fenichel, O. *The Psychoanalytic Theory of Neurosis*. New York: W. W. Norton & Company, Inc., 1945.

Ford, C. S., and Beach, F. A. *Patterns of Sexual Behavior*. New York: Harper and Brothers, Publishers, 1951.

Freud, S. "Three Contributions to the Theory of Sex." *The Standard Edition of the Complete Psychological Works of Sigmund Freud*. Vol. VII. London: Hogarth, 1953.

Friedman, P. "Sexual Deviations." *American Handbook of Psychiatry*. Vol. I (S. Arieti, ed.). New York: Basic Books, 1959.

Gutheil, E. A. "Sexual Dysfunctions in Men." *American Handbook of Psychiatry*. Vol. I (S. Arieti, ed.). New York: Basic Books, 1959.

Kinsey, A. C., et al. *Sexual Behavior in the Human Male*. Philadelphia: W. B. Saunders Company, 1948.

Kolb, L. C., and Johnson, A. M. "Etiology and Therapy of Overt Homosexuality." *Psychoanalyt. Quart.* 24:506, 1955.

Chapter 8

Aichhorn, A. *Wayward Youth*. New York: Viking Press, 1935.

Cleckley, H. *The Mask of Sanity*. St. Louis: C. V. Mosby Company, 1950.

Eissler, K. R. (ed.). *Searchlights on Delinquency*. New York: International Universities Press, 1949.

Giffin, M.; Johnson, A. M.; and Litin, E. H. "Specific Factors Determining Antisocial Acting Out." *Am. J. Orthopsychiat.* 24:664, 1954.

Glueck, S., and Glueck, E. *Physique and Delinquency*. New York: Harper and Brothers, Publishers, 1956.

Johnson, A. M., and Szurek, S. A. "The Genesis of Antisocial Acting Out in Children and Adults." *Psychoanalyt. Quart.* 21:323, 1952.

Johnson, A. M., "Juvenile Delinquency." *American Handbook of Psychiatry*. Vol I (S. Arieti, ed.). New York: Basic Books, 1959.

Lindner, R. *Rebel Without a Cause*. New York: Grune & Stratton, Inc., 1944.

Szurek, S. A. "Notes on the Genesis of Psychopathic Personality Trends." *Psychiatry*. 5:1, 1942.

Chapter 9

Anastasi, A. *Psychological Testing*. New York: Macmillan Company, 1954.

Buros, O. K. *The Fifth Mental Measurements Yearbook*. Highland Park, N.J.: Gryphon Press, 1959.

Cronbach, L. J. *Essentials of Psychological Testing*. New York: Harper and Brothers, Publishers, 1960.

Doll, E. "Notes on the Concept of Mental Deficiency." *Amer. J. Psychol.* 54:116, 1941.

Doll, E. A. *The Measurement of Social Competence.* Minneapolis: Educational Test Bureau, 1953.

Jervis, G. A. "The Mental Deficiencies." *American Handbook of Psychiatry.* Vol. II (S. Arieti, ed.). New York: Basic Books, 1959.

Terman, L. M., and Merrill, M. A. *Measuring Intelligence.* Boston: Houghton Mifflin Company, 1937.

Wechsler, D. *The Measurement and Appraisal of Adult Intelligence.* (4th ed.). Baltimore: Williams & Wilkins Company, 1958.

Chapter 10

Abse, D. W. "Hysteria." *American Handbook of Psychiatry.* Vol. I (S. Arieti, ed.). New York: Basic Books, 1959.

Brosin, H. W. "Psychiatric Conditions Following Head Injury." *American Handbook of Psychiatry.* Vol. II (S. Arieti, ed.). New York: Basic Books, 1959.

Goldstein, K. "Functional Disturbances in Brain Damage." *American Handbook of Psychiatry.* Vol. I (S. Arieti, ed.). New York: Basic Books, 1959.

Levin, M. "Toxic Psychoses." *American Handbook of Psychiatry.* Vol. II (S. Arieti, ed.). New York: Basic Books, 1959.

Wechsler, D. *The Measurement and Appraisal of Adult Intelligence.* (4th ed.). Baltimore: Williams & Wilkins Company, 1958.

Chapter 11

Arieti, S. *Interpretation of Schizophrenia.* New York: Brunner, 1955.

Cameron, N. "Paranoid Conditions and Paranoia." *American Handbook of Psychiatry.* Vol. I (S. Arieti, ed.). New York: Basic Books, 1959.

Freud, S. "Psycho-analytic Notes on an Autobiographical Account of a Case of Paranoia." *The Standard Edition of the Complete Psychological Works of Sigmund Freud.* Vol. XII. London: Hogarth, 1958.

Kitay, P., et al. "Symposium on 'Reinterpretation of the Schreber Case: Freud's Theory of Paranoia'." *Int. J. Psychoanal.* 44:191, 1963.

Klein, H. R., and Horwitz, W. A. "Psychosexual Factors in the Paranoid Phenomena." *Am. J. Psychiat.* 105:697, 1949.

Knight, R. P. "The Relationship of Latent Homosexuality to the Mechanism of Paranoid Delusions." *Bull. Menninger Clin.* 4:149, 1940.

Macalpine, I. and Hunter, R. (eds.) *Daniel Paul Schreber: Memoirs of My Nervous Illness.* London: Dawson, 1955.

Neiderland, W. G. "The 'Miracled-Up' World of Schreber's Childhood." *The Psychoanalytic Study of the Child.* Vol. XIV (R. Eissler, ed.). New York: International Universities Press, 1959.

Ovesey, L. "Pseudohomosexuality, the Paranoid Mechanism, and Paranoia." *Psychiatry.* 18:163, 1955.

Chapter 12

Arieti, S. *Interpretation of Schizophrenia.* New York: Brunner, 1955.
———— "Schizophrenia: The Manifest Symptomatology, the Psychodynamic and Formal Mechanisms." *American Handbook in Psychiatry.* Vol. I (S. Arieti, ed.). New York: Basic Books, 1959.

Bateson G.; Jackson, D. D.; Haley, J.; and Weakland, J. "Toward a Theory of Schizophrenia." *Behavioral Science.* 1:251, 1956.

Bellak, L. *Dementia Praecox.* New York: Grune and Stratton, Inc., 1948.

Bleuler, E. *Dementia Praecox, of the Group of Schizophrenias.* New York: International Universities Press, 1950.

Brody, E. B., and Redlich, F. C. (eds.). *Psychotherapy with Schizophrenics.* New York: International Universities Press, 1952.

Bruch, H. "Falsification of Bodily Needs and Body Concept in Schizophrenia." *Arch. Gen. Psychiat.* 6:18, 1962.

Cameron, N. *The Psychology of Behavior Disorders: A Biosocial Interpretation.* Boston: Houghton Mifflin Company, 1947.

Fromm-Reichmann, F. *Principles of Intensive Psychotherapy.* Chicago: University of Chicago Press, 1950.

Hoch, P., and Polatin, P. "Pseudoneurotic Forms of Schizophrenia." *Psychiatric Quarterly.* 23:248, 1949.

Kallmann, F. J. "The Genetic Theory of Schizophrenia." *Am. J. Psychiatry.* 103:309, 1946.

Lidz, R. W., and Lidz, T. "The Family Environment of Schizophrenic Patients." *Am. J. Psychiatry.* 106:332, 1949.

Niederland, W. G. "Further Data and Memorabilia Pertaining to the Schreber Case." *Int. J. Psychoanal.* 44:201, 1963.

Sullivan, H. S. *Conceptions of Modern Psychiatry.* New York: W. W. Norton & Company, Inc., 1953.

Chapter 13

Alexander, F., and French, T. *Psychoanalytic Therapy: Principles and Application.* New York: Ronald Press Co., 1946.

Arieti, S. *Interpretation of Schizophrenia.* New York: Brunner, 1955.

Fromm-Reichmann, F. *Principles of Intensive Psychotherapy.* Chicago: University of Chicago Press, 1950.

Kolb, L. C. "Psychotherapeutic Evolution and Its Implications." *Psychiat. Quart.* 30:579, 1956.

Munroe, R. L. *Schools of Psychoanalytic Thought*. New York: Dryden Press, 1955.

Rogers, C. *Client-Centered Therapy*. Boston: Houghton Mifflin Company, 1951.

Rogers, C., and Dymond, R. F. (eds.). *Psychotherapy and Personality Change*. Chicago: University of Chicago Press, 1954.

Sullivan, H. S. *The Interpersonal Theory of Psychiatry*. New York: W. W. Norton & Company, Inc., 1953.

Thompson, C. *Psychoanalysis: Evolution and Development*. New York: Hermitage House, 1950.

Wolberg, L. *The Technique of Psychotherapy*. New York: Grune & Stratton, Inc., 1954.

Index

abreaction, 139

acting out, antisocial, 83, 87; of punishment, 19; sexual, 73, 123

Adler, Alfred, 136n.

adolescence, changes in, 53; in psychiatric history, 147; in schizophrenia, 122

affect, defined, 139; inappropriate, 117; isolation of, 65–66; rigidity of, 117

affective disorder, defined, 139; *see also* depression

alcoholism, 80

alkalosis, respiratory, 33

ambivalence, 6; defined, 14, 139; lost object and, 14; obsessive behavior and, 58; in schizophrenia, 117; in weaning process, 17

amentia, 89

American Association on Mental Deficiency, 92

amnesia, 99; *see also* memory disorders

amoral behavior, 78, 84; *see also* antisocial behavior

anaclitic depression, 13

anal expulsion, 111, 112n.

anal stage, 111; defined, 139

anamnesis, 139

anesthesia, 46

anhedonia, 117, 124

animal research, 3n.

antisocial behavior, acting out of, 83, 87; factors in, 80–82; management of, 87–88

anxiety, castration, 73–74, 139; defenses against, 24–25; defined, 23, 139; discomfort of, 23, 30; displacement in, 37; as "disrespectable illness," 31; educative technique in, 33; environmental manipulation in, 32–33; "fight-flight" reaction in, 37; "heart attack" in, 33; homosexuality and, 73; hyperventilation syndrome in, 33; "irrational" nature of, 26,

30; management of, 31–34; mother-child relationships in, 28n.; neurosis, 8; neurotic vs. psychotic, 25; normal vs. abnormal, 24; organic disease and, 25; patient's dependency in, 34; physiological manifestations of, 23; psychodynamics of, 25–28; psychogenesis of, 28–30; regression and, 121; repression and, 27–28; states, 25, 29, 36

aphonia, 46

arachnodactyly, 93

arthritis, 47

association, phobic object and, 38

asthma, bronchial, 47

autism, 139

autoerotism, 139

"baby" role, 47

behavior, antisocial, *see* antisocial behavior; goal-directed, 2

Bellak Children's Apperception Test, 152

Bender, Lauretta, 153

Bender-Gestalt Test, 153

Binet, Alfred, 152

biochemical variations, in schizophrenia, 124

birth, anxiety and, 28n.

blank screen, therapist as, 132, 137

bodily expressions, psychodynamics of, 52–54; of psychological difficulties, 45–57

bodily functions, conversion symptoms and, 46

body, family and cultural communication about, 50–51, 54; role of in psychological difficulties, 49–50

body chemistry, schizophrenia and, 124

body-image, in psychological test, 153; schizophrenia and, 125, 127; sexual meaning of, 49

body-image disturbances, 48–49; management of, 55–57; psychogenesis of, 49–52
borderline patients, 137
bowel training, 61, 112; *see also* anal stage
brain damage, antisocial behavior and, 80–81; body-image and, 48
brain disorders, acute and chronic, 101–102; etiology of, 101–102; management of, 104
breast, "loss" of, 16–17, 50
bronchial asthma, 47

Campbell, R. J., 1n.
cardiovascular disease, 102
castration anxiety, 40, 73, 77; defined, 139
catatonia, 140
catatonic schizophrenia, 119, 144
catharsis, 140
cathexis, 140
cerebral arteriosclerosis, 102
cerebral defect, congenital, 93
cerebral lipoidosis, 93
character disorder, defined, 7–8, 140
cheating, chronic, 80
childhood experience, anxiety and, 26, 29; handsomeness or ugliness in, 51; in psychiatric history, 137
childhood phobias, 39–42
children, antisocial acting out in, 83; sexual assaults as cause of schizophrenia in, 126; *see also* parent
clang associations, 116
classification, defined, 2; illustrated, 5
cleanliness, obsessive, 65
Cleckley, H. M., 100n.
colitis, 47
communication disorders, schizophrenia and, 125–126
compartmentalization, 99
compulsion, 5; defined, 59, 140
confabulations, 98; defined, 140
conflict, 3, 140
conscience disorders, 78–88; management of, 87–88; psychodynamics of, 86–87; psychogenesis of, 81–86
consciousness, altered states of, 101; defined, 96
consciousness, disorders of, 96–104; organic, 98–99; psychodynamics and psychogenesis of, 102–104
constitutional factors, in conscience disorders, 81; in depressive reactions, 12; in schizophrenia, 124
conversion hysteria, 36
conversion reactions, defined, 46–47, 140; management of, 55
countertransference, 140

critical periods, in animal development, 3n.

decompensation, 140
defenses, defined, 140; vs. anxiety, 24–25; obsessive reactions and, 63–66; purpose of, 121n.
delinquent behavior, 81–83; *see also* antisocial behavior
delusion, 11; bodily, 49, 107; classification of, 106–107; defined, 105, 140; schizophrenia and, 116, 119, 126
dementia praecox, 118, 140; *see also* schizophrenia
denial, defined, 15, 140; in depressive reactions, 20; schizophrenia and, 126
dependency feelings, conversion reaction and, 46; gratification from, 123; phobias and, 40, 43; sexual disorders and, 72
depersonalization, 140
depression, 4–5; anaclitic, 13; defined, 9, 140; denial and, 15; exogenous vs. endogenous, 11–12; mania and, 15; neurotic, 8, 11; postpartum, 12–13; primary and secondary, 10–11; psychodynamics of, 6; psychotic, 5; as retroflexed rage, 14; as syndrome, 11; *see also* depressive reaction
depressive reaction, 9–22; clinging dependency on therapist, 21; as cry for help, 15–16, 19; incorporation in, 17–18; "lost object" and, 6, 14, 20; management of, 20–22; normal vs. pathological, 10; as punishment of other person, 19; psychodynamics of, 13–16; psychogenesis of, 16–19; spontaneous improvement in, 21; suicide and, 21–22; *see also* depression
dermatitis, atopic, 47
deterioration, 140
Deutsch, Helene, 4n., 5
displacement, 6; defined, 14, 37, 141
dissociation, 99, 144
Don Juanism, 71, 73; defined, 141
Draw-a-Person Test, 153
drug addiction, 80
drugs, in anxiety treatment, 32; in depression, 20–21; in mental retardation, 95; in paranoid conditions, 113; in phobic reactions, 44; in schizophrenia, 128

early life experiences, 6; anxiety and, 29; depressive reaction and, 16; importance of, 3; phobias and, 41, 44; *see also* childhood; parent-child relationships
echolalia, 141
ego boundaries, 17–18; defined, 50, 141; disturbances of, 117; schizophrenia and, 125, 127

electroconvulsive therapy, 21, 141
embolism, 102
emotion, defined, 141; visceral expression of, 47
empathy, 141
encephalitis, 101
encephalograms, air, 102
encephalopathy, 92–93
endocrine function, disequilibrium in, 12
English, Ava C., 1n.
English, H. B., 1n.
environment, body and, 49–50; manipulation of, 32–33, 135; epilepsy, hysterical, 101
erotomania, 109
euphoria, 141
exhibitionism, 69
experience, early life, *see* early life experience

family life, in psychiatric history, 147
fear, vs. anxiety, 23–24; normal vs. phobic, 36; *see also* phobias
feeblemindedness, 89–95
fetishism, 69, 141
fight-flight reaction, in anxiety, 37
fixation, 141
Fleschig, Paul Emil, 111
free association, 137, 141
Freud, Sigmund, 3n., 40, 108–110, 137
frustration, defined, 141; in learning process, 50n.
fugue states, 100
functional disorders, defined, 141; body-image and, 48–49; as learned reactions, 131; management of, 104
functional psychoses, 8; *see also* manic-depressive psychosis; schizophrenia

galactosemia, 93
gang delinquency, 82–83
gargoylism, 93
genetic factors, in depressive reactions, 12; mental retardation and, 89; in schizophrenia, 123–124
genital impulses, 28n.
grandeur, delusions of, 106
grandiosity, 141
grief (response), 4–6, 10, 13, 141
guilt feelings, 10–11, 88; amoral acts and, 79; anxiety and, 26–27; bodily functions and, 51; phobias and, 41

hallucinations, 11; defined, 141; schizophrenia and, 116, 119
Hans, Freud's case history of, 40
hate, vs. love, 64; *see also* ambivalence

"heart trouble," anxiety and, 33
Hinsie, L. E., 1n.
history, psychiatric, 146–149
homosexual act, in fugue state, 100; as "reparative," 74
homosexual impulses, anxiety and, 27
homosexual panic, 142
homosexuality, 69; denial of, 110; dependency in, 72; hostility reaction, 72; parental influences in, 84; preadolescence and, 71; unconscious, 73, 109
Horney, Karen, 136
hospitalization, in mental retardation, 91n.; in psychotic depression, 11; in schizophrenia, 128–129
hostility and hostility feelings, in antisocial behavior, 83; conversion reaction and, 46; overt, 80; "psychosomatic" disorder and, 47; reaction formation and, 64; in schizophrenia, 123; self-punishment for, 5–6; sexual disorders and, 71–72
hyperesthesia, 46
hypertension, 47
hyperventilation syndrome, 33
hypnosis, 43
hypochondriasis, 47–48, 109; defined, 142; management of, 56
hypothyroidism, 93
hysteria, 8; defined, 142; in conversion reactions, 46
hysterical epilepsy, 101

identification, 6; defined, 17–18, 142
idiot, 90
illness, as punishment, 51
illusion, 142
imbecile, 90
impotence, 70
impulse, 142
incorporation, 6; defined, 18, 142; in depressive reaction, 17–18
indifférence, in conversion reaction, 46
influence, delusions of, 107
insight, 142
insomnia, 9, 11, 48
insulin coma therapy, 128, 142
intellectual functioning, level of, 150; variability in, 91
Intelligence Quotient, 90–91, 142
intelligence tests, 152
interpersonal relationships, psychotherapy and, 137; in schizophrenia, 117, 122
interpretation, in psychotherapy, 132
interpretative psychotherapy, 136–137
intracranial infections, 101
introjection, 6; defined, 18–19, 142; in depressive reaction, 17–18
involutional melancholia, 12

involutional psychosis, 142
involuntary movement, 46
IQ, 90–91, 142
isolation, defined, 142; obsessive reactions and, 65–66

jealousy, 5, 109
Johnson, Adelaide, 83n.
Johnson-Szurek hypothesis, 83n., 85

kernicterus, 92

"la belle indifférence," 46, 142
Lawrence-Moon-Biedl syndrome, 93
limb amputation, 53–54, 57
loss, abnormal reaction to, 20; anxiety and, 26, 28n., 53; in depression, 13; fear of, 26; imagined, 14; incorporation and, 17
lost object, 6, 14, 20
love, vs. hate, 64; loss of, 26, 28n.; *see also* ambivalence
lying, chronic, 80

magical solution, in conversion reaction, 55; in depressive reaction, 16; in obsessive reaction, 63; in phobic reaction, 44
mania, defined, 142; denial and, 15
manic-depressive psychosis, 8, 12, 107, 142
masturbation, false beliefs about, 52, 75
megalomania, 109
melancholia, defined, 142; involutional, 12
memory, defined, 96
memory disorders, 48, 96–104; functional, 99–101; organic, 98–99; psychodynamics and psychogenesis of, 102–104
meningitis, 101
mental deficiency, 89; classification of, 90–91
mental distress, symptoms of, 1–2
mental retardation, 89–95; etiology of, 92; IQ and, 91; management of, 94–95; psychogenic, 94
mental status, in psychiatric history, 148
migraine, 47
Minnesota Multiphasic Personality Inventory, 152
mongolism, 93
Morgan, Christiana, 152
moron, 90
mother-child relationships, 6, 82; anxiety and, 28n.; schizophrenia and, 125
mothering relationship, anxiety and, 29; in depressive reactions, 16; in schizophrenia, 125
motivations, meaning and significance of, 5

motor function, loss of, 46
mourning, 10; *see also* depressive reaction
multiple personalities, 100, 103–104; schizophrenia and, 117
Murray, Henry, 152

neoplasm, intracranial, 93
neurodermatoses, 47
neurofibromatosis, 93
neurosis, defined, 7, 143
neurotic depression, 8, 11
nondirective psychotherapy, 132n.

obsession, 5; defined, 59, 143
obsessive-compulsive neurosis, 8, 60
obsessive personality, defined, 60
obsessive reactions, 58–67; defiance and, 61–62; isolation of affect in, 65; management of, 66–67; psychodynamics of, 62–66; psychogenesis of, 61–62; normal vs. pathological, 59–60; reaction formation in, 64; "undoing" in, 63
oedipal impulses, 28n., 40n., 143
oral ejection, 112
oral functions, constipation and, 19n., 20n.
oral stage, 16–19, 143
organic impairment, 150
orientation, defined, 96
orientation disorders, organic, 98–99; psychodynamics and psychogenesis of, 102–104; summary of, 96–104
overeating, depression and, 16

panic, 143
paralysis, 46
paranoia, as entity, 107; defined, 143
paranoid conditions, 105–114; management of, 113–114
paranoid delusions, psychodynamics of, 108–111
paraplegia, 46
parent, moral code of, 84–85; phobic, 44; schizophrenic behavior and, 126; symbolic, 38
parent-child relationships, antisocial behavior and, 82–84, 88; identification in, 18; in obsessive reactions, 61–62; phobias and, 40–41; re-living of, 131
paresthesia, 46
penis envy, 74
persecution, delusions of, 106
perseveration, 98, 150
personality, multiple, 100, 103–104
personality tests, 151
phenylketonuria, 93
phobia, defined, 35, 143; intimidation and satisfaction in, 39; vs. normal fears, 36; sexual aspect of, 40n.

phobias and phobic reactions, 35–44; management of, 43–44; psychodynamics of, 36–40; psychogenesis of, 41–42; withdrawal in, 41–42
phobic neurosis, 8
phobic object, choice of, 37–38
phobic reactions, vs. phobias, 36; *see also* phobias and phobic reactions
physiological complaints and symptoms, classification of, 45–49
possessions, overvaluation of, 62
postpartum depression, 12–13
premature ejaculation, 70
projection, defined, 108, 143; mechanism of, 110–111; phobias and, 42; schizophrenia and, 126
projective techniques, 143, 151
pseudohomosexual anxiety, 73
pseudoneurotic schizophrenia, 61, 145
psoriasis, 47
psychiatric history, outline for, 146–149
psychiatry, 143
psychoanalysis, defined, 143; psychodynamics and, 7; as psychotherapy, 136–137
psychoanalyst, 143
psychodynamics, basic assumption of, 2–3; case history and, 4–6; defined, 2, 143
psychogenesis, assumptions concerning, 6; defined, 3; therapy and, 7
psychological difficulties, bodily expression of, 45–57
psychological testing, 150–153
psychologist, 144
psychoneurosis, 144
psychopath, 2n.; defined, 144
psychopathic personality, 2n., 81
psychopathologist, 144
psychopathology, defined, 1
"psychopathy," 2n.; early life experiences and, 3–4
psychophysiological disorders, 47, 56
psychosis, defined, 7, 144; in obsessive behavior, 60; functional, 7; *see also* manic-depressive psychosis; schizophrenia
psychosomatic disorders, 47, 54–55; defined, 144; management of, 56
psychotherapy, common elements in, 133–134; defined, 144; fantasied vs. reality experience in, 133; general rationale for, 130–138; interpretative, 132, 134–138; "nondirective" type, 132; supportive, 132, 134–138

Rado, S., 136n.
rage, defiance and, 61–62; undoing process and, 63–64
rationalization, 144

reaction formation, defined, 64, 144
reference, delusions of, 106
regression, defined, 144; in schizophrenia, 121
Reik, Theodor, 136n.
repression, anxiety and, 30–31; conversion reaction and, 46; defined, 27, 144; displacement and, 37; phobias and, 42; in sexual disorders, 75–76
"rescue fantasy," suicide attempts and, 21
resistance, 144
Rorschach, Hermann, 152
Rorschach test, 152

schizophrenia, 8, 20n., 115–129; altered states of consciousness in, 101; anhedonia in, 124; areas and symptoms of, 116–117; biochemical variations in, 124; body chemistry in, 124; body-image and, 125; borderline, catatonic, 119; classification of, 118–120; defined, 115–116, 144–145; ego-boundary disturbance in, 117; genetic influences in, 123–124; hebephrenic, 119; hostility in, 123; interpersonal relationships and, 122; latent, 120; management of, 128–129; paranoid, 107, 112, 119; physiological influences in, 124; "process" vs. "reactive," 118; pseudoneurotic, 61, 120; psychodynamics of, 121–123; psychogenesis of, 123–127; psychological factors in, 124–127; regression in, 121; simple, 118; social recovery in, 128–129; tranquilizers in, 128
schizophrenogenic mother, 125
school, phobias about, 40; rebellion against, 62
Schreber, Dr. Daniel, case of, 108–111, 126
secondary gain, in conversion reactions, 46; defined, 145
seizures, in conversion reactions, 46
self-esteem, anxiety and, 31; hypochondriasis and, 48; loss of, 10–11; phobias and, 41
self-identity, 6, 17–18; in schizophrenia, 117, 123, 125
senile psychosis, 145
sensation, altered, 46
Sentence Completion Test, 153
sexual disorders, 68–78; classification of, 69–71; dependency in, 72; hostility in, 71–72; management of, 77–78; misplaced identification and, 74; psychodynamics of, 71–74; psychogenesis of, 74–76; repression and, 75–76
sexual impulses, anxiety and, 27–28; conversion reaction and, 46; phobias and, 40n.

sexual meaning, in body-image disturb-
    ances, 49
shock treatment, 145
sickness, body concept in, 50–51; as "sin,"
    51
"signal anxiety," 29
sociopathic, 145
suicide, 21–22; risk detected in tests, 151
Sullivan, Harry Stack, 136n.
superego, as conscience, 82; defined, 145;
    nondeveloped, 86; of parents, 85
suppression, 145
surgical trauma, 53–54
Stanford-Binet Intelligence Scales, 152
stealing, 80
Sturge-Weber-Dimitri's disease, 93
symptom, defined, 2; function of, 135;
    study of, 1–2
syphilis, 102
systemic infections, 101–102
Szurek, S. A., 83n.

tachycardia, paroxysmal, 47
Tay-Sach's disease, 93
temper tantrums, 62
Thematic Apperception Test, 152
therapist, requirements and qualifications
    of, 131–132; transference and, 131
Thigpen, C. H., 100n.
thought processes, breakdown of in schizo-
    phrenia, 116
Three Faces of Eve, 100
tics, 46, 62
tranquilizers, in anxiety, 32; in mental re-
    tardation, 95; in schizophrenia, 128

transference, 131, 145
transvestism, 70, 85
traumas, in brain disorders, 101; in schizo-
    phrenia, 126; surgical, 53
treatment, forms of, 6–7; *see also* therapist;
    psychotherapy
tremors, 46
truancy, 80
tuberous sclerosis, 93

ulcer, peptic, 47
unconscious, 145
"undoing," of castration, 74; defined, 63,
    145

vaginismus, 70
ventriculography, 102
Vineland Social Maturity Scale, 90
vomiting, 23, 31, 35, 112n.
von Recklinghausen's disease, 93
voyeurism, 69, 72, 75

war neuroses, 26
weaning, reaction to, 16–17
Wechsler Adult Intelligence Scale, 98n.,
    152
Wechsler Intelligence Scale for Children,
    152
withdrawal, phobias and, 41–42; in schizo-
    phrenia, 122
"word salad," 116

x-rays, of skull, 102